ARTFUL DODGING

Also by Jeanne Martinet

The Art of Mingling
Getting Beyond "Hello"
The Faux Pas Survival Guide
Come-Ons, Comebacks, and Kiss-Offs

ARTFUL DODGING

Painless Techniques
for Avoiding Anyone Anytime

Jeanne Martinet

ST. MARTIN'S GRIFFIN ☙ NEW YORK

www.stmartins.com

Book design by Jane Adele Regina

Library of Congress Cataloging-in-Publication Data

Martinet, Jeanne.
    Artful dodging : painless techniques for avoiding anyone anytime / Jeanne Martinet.
        p. cm.
    ISBN 0-312-25460-1
    1. Interpersonal relations.   2. Interpersonal communication.
3. Etiquette.   I. Title.

HM132.M3457 2000
302—dc21   00-027844

First Edition: June 2000

10   9   8   7   6   5   4   3   2   1

CONTENTS

Acknowledgments

I would like to thank everyone who has ever dodged me artfully enough that I remained blissfully ignorant of it. I would also like to thank those people who unwittingly allowed me to practice my dodging techniques on them. If, however, you are a friend or relative of mine who suspects me of having dodged you at one time or or another, I swear to you I never did. (Anyway, that's my story, and I'm sticking to it.)

The Myth of "Just Say No"

It was right before Thanksgiving, and the increasing demands of life had begun to cause some serious cracks around the edges of my personality. I had just said good-bye to one houseguest and was expecting another in a week. My editor was clamoring for a manuscript I hadn't finished. My relatives had been calling to schedule not only Thanksgiving events but also various Christmas get-togethers. My cat had an eye infection and I hadn't found the time to take him to the vet. Unpaid bills and other paperwork were piled high on my desk. To top it all off with one big stressful cherry, I was getting the flu. In short, I felt as if every moment of every day had become a negotiation— a battle between my survival and the needs and desires of people around me.

One evening I came home tired and laden down with groceries. When the elevator came, I was relieved to have it all to myself. I was in no mood for chitchat and wanted nothing more than to get into my apartment, where I could put my bags down and my feet up. Then, just as the elevator door was closing, an arm snaked its way into the opening. As if I were in a horror film, I watched the arm force the elevator door back open, revealing an upstairs neighbor who had taken to waylaying me in the elevator on a daily basis. She had just finished writing her first novel and—due to some vague encouraging noises I had made six months before—had designated me to be the lucky one to introduce it to the rest of the world. (P.S. There were already four manuscripts from various friends sitting on my bedside table.)

"Hi!" she greeted me exuberantly as we started going up, "I was hoping I would run into you! I've got my manuscript right here—so now I don't even have to mail it to you." She pointed to a bulging bag at her side. It looked like a 500-pager at least.

It was at that moment that something inside me snapped. I shook my head violently at her and kind of moaned. "My god—what's wrong with you?" she asked me.

"I'm sorry, I just *can't*," I said.

"Can't? Can't what?"

"Can't read your manuscript."

"But . . . it's not that long," pleaded the woman. "Couldn't you just . . ."

"NO!" I heard myself say much too loudly as I got off the elevator, leaving my poor neighbor standing there with her mouth open. Believe me, it was not my finest hour, and I did my best to put the episode out of my mind.

One week later my houseguest and I arrived at my building soaked through from a freezing rain and eager to get inside my warm apartment. As we ran for the elevator I saw that this same neighbor was already inside the car. "Hold the elevator, please!" I called.

She smiled coldly at me. "I'm sorry, I just CAN'T," she said as the door closed in our dripping and dismayed faces. My houseguest was understandably annoyed. But I was ashamed.

It was at that moment that I resolved never to hurt someone unnecessarily like that again.

It would be a lovely thing if we lived in a world where we could just say no to anything that came our way when we'd rather it hadn't. In such a world, we could tell our obnoxious in-laws we don't feel like coming to their house for dinner, period. We could tell irate bosses we haven't finished our work and that's that. We could tell bores at cocktail parties we don't want to listen to them talk anymore, and blind dates from hell that we are going home early because we don't like them. In other words, we could speak our minds, the way small children do, without using any protective filter. (Actually there are some adults who do this without giving it a second thought. Unfortunately, with the exception of those few who are spiritually advanced enough to project a special love energy during the act of rejection, these people are social imbeciles.) But the truth is that the fabric of society is held together by an intricate weaving of deceptions and subterfuges.

I confess I am sometimes accused (mostly by Californians) of being a sneaky, insincere sort of person—merely because many of my social strategies and solutions happen to be based on lying. These idealists believe that we would all be better off if everyone just told the truth. I watched one of these "Honest Abes" in action at a barbecue in Upstate New York one weekend. He was standing with me and a friend of mine when a woman approached, calling the Honest Abe by name. As the woman leaned forward for a greeting kiss, Abe put out his hand and said crisply, "I'd rather not kiss. Let's just shake hands."

The newcomer was visibly embarrassed. I was embarrassed

for her. My friend was also embarrassed. We all stood there awkwardly while the proposed handshake took place. The chagrined woman chatted with us for a minute but left as soon as she could. When she was gone I asked Abe just what the heck was going on between him and the would-be kisser. Abe told me that they were acquaintances, that there was no history or relationship between them. He went on to explain that he had been merely practicing his new policy of total honesty. Apparently Abe didn't care for greeting kisses, and he was quite proud of his newfound ability to clearly communicate his needs and feelings.

I had to bite my tongue (not a wise thing to do while eating spicy barbecue) to keep from asking Abe what had happened to his manners. Self-realization and personal integrity notwithstanding, how hard would it have been for Abe to have sacrificed his dedication to the truth just enough to add "I think I'm catching a cold" to his rebuff? Better yet, it would have been a fairly simple matter for him to have physically parried the kiss and just shaken the woman's hand without making any sort of verbal confrontation out of it. Too many people today pride themselves on being able to say no when they mean no. Gone are the elegant Victorian practices of subtle rejections and delicate deferment, designed to sound more like compliments and self-deprecations than like rebuffs. Decades of social changes, psychotherapy, twelve-step programs, encounter groups, and communication seminars have trained people to be more direct in expressing their feelings and desires. But somewhere along the way we lost something very important. Certain social skills have been forgotten, and honesty has become a highly overrated commodity.

Don't get me wrong. I *am* in favor of truth-telling when it comes to marriage counseling, court appearances, and IRS audits. But when one of your good friends suggests a play date between your darling little Johnny and her cute little Lizzie, which you would rather die than arrange as cute little Lizzie happens to be a foul-mouthed face biter, the truth is not usually a good option. What good is the truth going to do you when your old buddy from college calls you up to borrow money you know there's not a chance in a million he'll ever pay back? How are you going to handle it when you realize you made two lunch dates by mistake and they are both waiting for you at the same restaurant? What can you do if you simply want the person standing in front of you to go away, to stop talking—or even to disappear entirely from your life?

Most of us have too many demands on our time and energy. We jump when the phone rings, cringe when the office door opens, and dread hearing words like "I wonder if you could possibly . . . ?" Whether we are confronted by a meddling mother, an obsessed ex-boyfriend, a busybody on the bus, or a needy client, we would often give anything to be able to come up with a smooth and effective, socially acceptable escape. Having good techniques for getting away—or staying away—from people who are interfering with our work life or leisure time is as important to our well-being as having the cleverest come-on lines or the most powerful negotiating skills.

Sometimes, of course, you *can* just say no. But not that often. An unvarnished "No" can hurt another person's feelings and may even cause inconvenient psychological fallout to you (things like begging, crying, yelling, disinheriting, firing, or punching). It is therefore surprising that most people, when suddenly faced with an unappealing something or someone, have no idea how to get out of the situation gracefully. "I've got a headache," "The cat threw up on it," and "My grandmother died," will take you only so far, after all, and a poorly executed or ill-chosen dodge can be much worse than no dodge at all. If you are using the same dodge on your old high school pal as you are on a door-to-door vacuum-cleaner salesman, you are probably not convincing anyone.

There have been countless books written about how to talk to people—how to flirt, network, make friends, get dates, or get jobs; how to be pursued, picked up, praised, promoted, or popular. But I have found that it is frequently harder to say good-bye than to say hello. Harder to dump a date than to go on one. In fact, it is almost always harder to say no than yes. And while there are a few natural born dodgers in the world (most of them end up in politics), the rest of us tend to need a little help. Dodging is an art form, like dance, and if you don't know the steps you can smash your partner's toe or stumble and fall flat on your face.

The techniques and strategies in this book can enable you to stay home from out-of-town weddings, conventions, or other events that you have no desire to attend. They can empower you to evade your eccentric office mate when she invites you over (again!) for dinner. You'll learn the best way to blow off bores, bums, or bullies; shun sexual advances; oust houseguests and turn down unwanted gifts; faze out friends; bail out of bad dates or tedious parties; duck family get-togethers; fend off fanatics, and even (shhh . . .) skip out on checks. You'll be given step-by-step instructions on how to circumvent favor seekers, sidestep sticky issues, bypass blame, avert intrusive personal questions, extricate yourself from arguments, temporarily table tough assignments, excoriate ex-lovers, or even—the ultimate dodge—totally vanish from someone's life.

Much of the power we have exists in the boundaries we set for ourselves. It is inevitable that we are going to have to reject certain things that come our way; we can do it awkwardly and ineffectively or we can do it with finesse. Ultimately, being able to dodge people so that they don't know we are doing it is a skill that safeguards everyone's emotional equilibrium. And as it was for Charles Dickens's infamous Artful Dodger, the better you are at your craft the less likely it is that you will ever get caught. The talented pickpocket in *Oliver Twist* would have his hand in and out of a gentleman's pocket so quickly— and in so deft a manner—that the gentleman never was sure exactly where he had lost the pocket's contents; at the same time the Dodger was so good at disappearing in a crowd and at eluding the police that he was virtually invulnerable. While thievery is probably not your objective, this kind of effortless evasion is.

One day not too long ago I was talking to a bleary-eyed, stressed-out lawyer, a partner in a busy New York firm. His workload was getting to him and he was threatening to rip the phone out of the wall in his office. "People keep asking me for things—for help or advice—all the time," he wailed. "I can't get my own work done! I am getting more and more behind every day."

I was incredulous. It is always amazing to me how many people in positions of power do not seem to have control over their day-to-day lives. "But if you're a partner, can't you just say no to them?" I asked him.

"These are people I just can't say no to," was his response. "They know I have the information they need."

"Well then, why don't you just dodge some of them?" I suggested, still puzzled.

"You mean . . . hide from them? Lie to them?"

"Exactly."

He looked at me as if I had just suggested he hold up a convenience store. "Oh, I wouldn't feel right about that. I don't like being dishonest."

I managed to refrain from making the obvious comment about honesty and lawyers, and I let the matter drop. But when I saw him again two weeks later, he looked like death itself. His skin was pasty, his clothes were wrinkled, and his expression wild. "Okay," he said without preamble, "teach me how to dodge."

Artful Dodging

CHAPTER 1

The Ethics of Evasion

Too much truth
Is uncouth.
—FRANKLIN PIERCE ADAMS

A funny thing happened to me on the way to writing this book, something that has rarely happened to me before. I had trouble getting people to talk to me. When I asked them to tell me about their dodging experiences, most people displayed varying degrees of uneasiness. Some stared blankly or laughed nervously; many claimed they never dodged—never equivocated, never evaded. (Some interviewees even changed the subject and *dodged the interview* entirely!) Although almost everyone told me he or she could really use this book and couldn't *wait* to read it, very few people would admit to ever having dodged anyone else.

What was surprising to me about this is that whenever I have written about social interaction, my readers have always been more interested in the subject of escape than in anything else. The fear of being stuck somewhere unpleasant—whether it is in an actual corner at a party or in a figurative corner fielding a request from someone—seems to be uppermost in people's minds. And yet somewhere along the line folks got the idea that it was unethical, immoral, or just plain cowardly not to deal with everyone directly and honestly. Like sex throughout much of history, dodging is something we all secretly do but feel ashamed of. Even the white lie—which used to be an accepted sign of good breeding and a sensitive nature—is now widely considered somehow unhealthy, even pernicious.

For some people, the term "dodger" conjures up the image of a sort of sniveling, sneaking snake in the grass who is trying to shirk his responsibilities (as in draft dodger); or a heartless power monger with a cell phone growing out of his ear who feels he needs to cut a swath through the bothersome demands on his time and energy. This is a misconception. Artful or non-artful, most of the world's dodging is done by nice, normal people like you. It is an inevitable fact of life.

Of course, by "dodging" I mean navigating smoothly around life's minor obstacles. I do not mean lying on your résumé, avoiding your civic duty, or hiding from the police. So before we discuss specific techniques, let's talk about what's right and what's wrong in the world of evasion.

TO FLEE OR NOT TO FLEE: WHEN TO DODGE

There are two basic motives for dodging people: to protect oneself or to protect someone else (or a combination of both).

So let's take a look at what triggers your dodging impulse *(and whether or not you should follow it)*:

ALTRUISM: Let's say you really love friend X but your husband went ahead and invited X's archenemy, Y, to your cocktail party before you could stop him. Rather than hurt X's feelings by telling her Y has been invited to your house—and rather than run the risk of X's coming and having an encounter of a toxic kind with Y—you feel you should somehow hide the fact of the party from X. *(This is the noblest reason for dodging—to protect another person. Good for you for going to the trouble!)*

SEMI-ALTRUISM: You found a certain blind date unappetizing, even though she is a perfectly nice person. The problem: She seems to have taken quite a shine to you. You don't want to see her again but would rather she didn't know it's because she's flat-chested and dresses like your mother. *(By all means, gently dodge her. In this case you are protecting the suitor's feelings and at the same time extricating yourself from an unwanted entanglement.)*

SELF-DEFENSE: You went out with him twice before discovering he is a member of a white supremist group and has an extensive collection of guns and Victoria's Secret catalogs. When he said good-bye after your last dinner he grabbed your thigh and called you his "personal honey pot." *(Dodge, baby, dodge! Your only choice here, dodging is often done sheerly for survival. If you try to tell this psychotic Neanderthal the truth—that you think you should call it quits because you have nothing in common—he's liable to make it his life's work to convince you otherwise. Stalkers are no fun to deal with.)*

FACE-SAVING: You are a sales rep. One of your important buyers comes to see you in your office—an unexpected drop-by. Since you don't want this buyer to see that you have only a dingy cubicle instead of a grand corner office, you are tempted to instruct your assistant to tell the buyer you are out at a meeting. *(Do it. Image is everything in the corporate world).* When you get home you realize you have a date—arranged weeks ago—with an old boyfriend who is in town on business. You are very fond of this man but don't particularly want him to see you in your current physical state, which is fifteen pounds overweight with a blemish the size of Mount Rushmore on your chin. You consider calling him and telling him you have the flu. *(A perfectly reasonable dodging impulse. While it may not be the most courageous avenue to take, not wanting to lose someone's good opinion of you is a common reason for dodging. Other face-saving motives include not wanting someone to find out you didn't get a job or raise, not wanting someone to know you've been fired, not wanting someone to see that your apartment is poorly kept or poorly decorated, or not wanting someone to discover that you are the world's worst cook. Face-saving dodges are about preserving status.)*

BUTT COVERING: Your boss is on the warpath because you haven't finished the report you were supposed to have on her desk first thing in the morning. A customer calls to demand an overdue refund check, which is not ready. Another customer is hounding you for some sales figures you said you'd have by today. A coworker is bugging you for a trade publication you borrowed and have misplaced somewhere. *(Just an average day in the lives of 90 percent of America. Most people couldn't survive without dodging at* *least some of the time. This is why when people tell you they never lie, they are lying.)*

PROTECTING YOUR PRIVACY: You've decided to become a recluse in order to work on your novel. You don't want anyone to know what you are really doing in case it turns out you can't write after all. In fact, when you do find out you are no Ernest Hemingway, you become very depressed and decide that until the Prozac kicks in you would rather not socialize with anyone. *(You are always within your rights to guard your personal space. In other words it's okay to choose to dodge people when telling the truth is too hard, too complicated, too private, too revealing, or too scandalous for public consumption.)*

HEDGING YOUR BETS: You are an administrator in city government. A brash young man comes to see you, to apply for an internship for which he is clearly not qualified by either experience, education, or temperament. However, you happen to notice on his résumé that he seems very well connected, probably through his family. Do you tell him the bald truth—that he is not at all right for the job? *(I wouldn't. You never know; in two or three years this whippersnapper could be running the town, and you along with it. Better to tell him he's one of your top candidates and then let him down gently later. Remember that dodging can shield you from potentially harmful repercussions—now or in the future.)*

TIME SAVING: You walk into an electronics store to buy a new CD player. You've got exactly twenty-five minutes to choose one, pay for it, and get back to the office. A store employee who looks like he's sixteen years old asks if he can help you. The guy seems nice enough but not too well endowed in the brains department. You hesitate. You don't want to be rude, but you really would rather another person wait on you. *(Dodging was invented for just these little life emergencies. Even if the person waiting on you is knowledgeable he may be disagreeable. You have a right to expect your retail experience to be both efficient and pleasant—after all, you are the customer—but neither is it acceptable or advisable to insult someone. There are several easy ways to dodge the salesperson and find someone else.)*

BOREDOM AND OTHER PSYCHOLOGICAL DISCOMFORTS: It's happened to everyone. I call it the Great Glaze Out. You get invited to a lecture given by your accountant's husband; what they failed to tell you until you are already there is that it was going to be three hours long and on the subject of duck hunting on the Eastern Shore. Or you get cornered at a party by the dullest person on earth—maybe in the whole solar system—who answers every one of your barely polite questions with a long monologue of excruciating details and is oblivious to be your darting eyes, which betray your silent scream of "Get me out of here, someone!" *(It's definitely okay to dodge bores, pests, pontificators, mashers, drunks, and fanatics. Sometimes you can just dodge the subject without having to dodge the person entirely. But whether it's a bad date or a bad presentation, there's no reason you can't leave when you want, as long as you are courteous in doing so. That's what artful dodging is all about. On the other hand, if you find most of the world too tiresome to talk to you might want to take a hard look at yourself.)*

FEAR AND PARANOIA: You were fired unfairly and are bringing a lawsuit against your former employer. She is a powerful and vindictive woman who is not happy about the situation, to say the least. So you sit at home refusing to answer the phone in case it might be her calling—or one of her lackeys. In fact, you're not really sure who is on your side. The safest thing, you tell yourself, is to talk to no one. *(This kind of fear is not a healthy motivation for dodging and can negatively affect your life. Similarly, you should also never dodge due to a past trauma; just because back in 1980 you had a bad experience with a neighbor who turned out to be a Peeping Tom doesn't mean you should avoid all your neighbors. Don't dodge a party just because you won't know anybody. Don't dodge a blind date because you are afraid you won't know what to talk about. In general, never dodge when you are nervous about something that is potentially rewarding.)*

DOUBLE BOOKING: You hate being alone Saturday night, so you make two dates on the same night just to be certain you've got it covered. When your number-one choice confirms, you call your backup date and cancel. *(Who are you, an airline? You can't bump people. Don't abuse your dodging tactics when you don't really need them.)*

LAZINESS: You said you would help out at the community center on Saturday but when the time comes you realize you'd rather watch the Mets game. When the center calls you tell them your kid's sick and you can't come. *(Bad move. Dodging is not ethical in this case, and TV should never take the place of real life.)*

REVENGE: Years ago he broke your heart into a million pieces. You never really knew what happened to him until one day you walk into a meeting at work and he is introduced to you as the new liaison for the West Coast branch of your company. Later that week, he calls your office to get some information he badly needs. You think about how satisfying it would be to dodge him, just to cause him trouble. *(There is no law against dodging under these circumstances, but trust me, you will not feel good afterward. This kind of dodging is extremely bad for your karma and is the sort of thing that only turns out well if you are the heroine in a Jacqueline Susann novel.)*

Ultimately, only you can decide when you should dodge and when you shouldn't. In some cases it may make you feel better to face whatever it is head-on. Sometimes you simply won't have the energy to dodge; you'll go through with something you thought was going to be horrible and it will turn out fine. Then there are the times when dodging can really liberate you, or save you from a fate worse than death. If you are confused about whether or not to dodge, it might help to repeat the Dodging Serenity Prayer:

"God grant me the serenity to accept the things I cannot dodge, the courage to dodge what I can, and the wisdom to know the difference."

SHEDDING YOUR GUILT

When I was doing research for this book, I spoke with a former acquisitions editor who suffered from severe dodger's guilt.

Every day, she told me, dozens of manuscripts and proposals would land on her desk. After being logged in, they were added to the mountain of manuscripts already piled high on her shelves. In addition to all the usual office pressures and demands of paperwork, meetings, and bosses, agents and authors would call throughout the day—each expecting and/or demanding that the consideration of his manuscript be her top priority. She was always way behind; it was the nature of the publishing business. And so, naturally, she dodged. And she dodged. In fact, she claimed she spent about 40 percent of her day circumnavigating people who were begging her, threatening her, or trying to bribe her to put their material first. And unlike many other editors, she felt very guilty having to dodge people. She could never get used to it.

The editor started having a recurring nightmare. Several times a month she dreamed that she was in her office looking for a misplaced manuscript. Suddenly she would realize there were people hiding behind the wall where the manuscripts were stacked. She would run for the door, but not before the authors-turned-monsters had tackled her. One day, after having this dream the night before, the editor found herself unable to effectively dodge an important, tough-to-handle agent. "I'm . . . I'm sorry," she broke down and confessed to him on the phone, "I know I've had it for weeks, but I haven't read it." She was close to tears and knew the agent could hear how upset she was.

"*Dar*-ling," the agent soothed, "it's only a manuscript—don't have a nervous breakdown over it!" The editor was surprised and grateful at this unexpected turn of events. She had anticipated yelling and screaming.

"Okay . . . thanks, Joe," she laughed, breathing easily again.

"So I'll expect an answer by tomorrow," he barked, and hung up. (Shortly thereafter, the editor left publishing and became a massage therapist.)

Before performing an artful dodge of any kind, you must first eliminate the presence of any guilt. Feeling guilty about telling someone you are in a meeting when you are not is like feeling guilty about choosing one entree out of dozens on the menu. You can't eat everything in one sitting, and you can't respond to everyone when and how they want you to. There is a word for people who say yes to absolutely everyone, anytime: nymphomaniac. So why do we feel so bad for ducking things?

There are usually two reasons we feel guilty avoiding something that someone else wants us to do: 1) from the other person's point of view it is appropriate and desirable that we do this particular something; therefore we feel the pressure of their reality (in other words, we think maybe the other person is right), and 2) with the exception of the very rich and the very powerful, we have all been on the other side of a dodge and know how it feels to be rejected, deflected, avoided, or ignored. It doesn't feel good.

To get over the guilt/fear/shame hurdle, it is essential for you to remember that the game of dodging is one that everybody plays. The object of the game is to play it well, so that you get where you are going and do it with the least possible amount of wave making. You are the master of ceremonies of your life; choices have to be made—by you. Once you accept that a certain amount of rejection is a part of modern life, then you will begin to feel guilty *only if you dodge sloppily*. Becoming more proficient in the art of dodging will actually make you a nicer, more socially evolved person.

To dodge well, you need to focus—with all the attention of a fine craftsman—on the task at hand, which is to protect yourself as well as the ego of the other person. Guilt is just going to get in your way. For one thing, it will almost certainly affect your believability. (I don't know about you, but it makes my whole face turn a funny color.) Like animals who can smell fear, people can sense guilt, and the guiltier you feel the more likely you are to get caught in a dodge. For another thing, guilt takes up a lot of psychic energy. And you are going to need all your energy for dodging brilliantly.

If you find you absolutely cannot shed your guilt about saying no to your brother-in-law's offer of free salsa lessons, it will probably be better for you to just get out your dancing shoes and let him whirl you around the floor than to feel ashamed of yourself every time you hear a rumba on the radio. However, I strongly encourage you to give yourself permission to shed your guilt. In most cases, guilt is unproductive, unhealthy, and un-called for.

Unless, of course, you commit one of the seven dodging sins.

THE SEVEN DODGING SINS

Whatever technique you use when you dodge, you must make every effort not to commit any of the following transgressions. Doing so will undermine your social and spiritual health—and land you in the dodger's doghouse.

1. NOT RETURNING PHONE CALLS: Many people seem to think that the modern practice of not returning phone calls is a

valid, if passive, dodging technique. I have one word for these people: unacceptable. Whenever someone commits this sin with me (and if she knows me at all she doesn't dare) I am appalled that the person considers this a viable option. I agree that not dealing with a problem and hoping it will just go away can be tempting, especially when it's someone calling to ask you for one of the three precious personal commodities: time, effort, or money. But in my opinion, failing to return a phone call on purpose is a rude, mean, and completely unnecessary breach of manners. It also makes people mad, thereby compounding the problem. (It is my secret belief that somewhere in the hidden psyche of all mass murderers you will find anger at an unreturned phone call.) Not only that, but it's inefficient as a dodging strategy; invariably the person will call back at least one more time to make certain you got her message. All you've done is to delay the issue, not solve it. If you really loathe the idea of talking to the person, often the call can be acknowledged by E-mail ("Got home too late to return your call—thought I'd E-mail you. Sorry to say will be busy all month") or you can let some time pass before calling back (see the Slowdown, page 88).

There are some exceptions to this strict call-back rule. If the caller is someone who has been harassing you, or you suspect he is a card-carrying psychopath, you may ignore the call. A stranger who calls you at home with no personal reference need not be called back. Wrong numbers don't have to be called back; still, if the messages they are leaving seem urgent it can be a generous act on your part to let the callers know of their error. If you are in mourning or in the midst of some other major life crisis (and I don't mean a bad hair day) your lapse can be forgiven also.

In addition, there are some businesses that elicit a huge volume of calls from strangers. Often it is an impossibility to get back to everyone, although I maintain that a good business is one which has a system for dealing with these kinds of calls. I have a friend who is a reporter for a major newspaper. He told me that unlike many of his colleagues, he makes it a habit to return the "nut" calls. He says it's important to wade through the crazies, because one of those calls could be a great story just waiting to be found. (Note: After the caller tells him that aliens have planted radio transmitters in her brain, she becomes a dodgeable caller.)

2. STANDING SOMEONE UP: No one should do this. Not showing up without calling goes way beyond dodging. It's okay to fail to show up at a large party or meeting—anything where the event is not ruined by your absence—as long as you apologize convincingly later (see Chapter 4).

3. FAILING TO R.S.V.P.: This may seem like a minor point of etiquette but the very fact that it is such a small and easy thing is why I consider it a sin. If there is an R.S.V.P. date requested, make every effort to observe it; however, even if you call the day before the affair, you *absolutely must* respond to a written invitation. Not doing so is like saying, "Even though you were thoughtful enough to mail me an invitation and you like me enough to want me to come to your party, you are not worth a one-minute phone call from me." Furthermore, a host needs to know how many guests to expect. Forget to R.S.V.P. too many times and you may find people start forgetting to invite you.

4. DODGING BIG STUFF: Artful Dodging does not mean cheating on your taxes, your wife, or your homework. Lying about any-

thing important (like whether you are married or have a contagious disease) to anybody important in your life (your mate, your kids, your best friend, your parole officer) is not recommended. Far be it from me to encourage anyone to acts of depravity or criminality. Don't forget that for the most part, dodging is for getting out of your sister-in-law's third(!) baby shower or that Tuesday lunch with the loudmouthed cardboard-box supplier.

5. BREAKING A PROMISE: What constitutes breaking a promise? As childish as this definition may seem, breaking a promise is when you have actually said the words, "I promise," and then you don't come through. If the dodge you are thinking of perpetrating means you are going to break a promise to someone, it is bad for your reputation to do so. (In other words, if it means breaking a promise, your grandmother had better *really* be dead this time.)

6. ACUSING SOMEONE OF DODGING YOU: I must admit to having committed this dodging sin a few times in my life, so I speak from hard-won experience. If you are smart—and have some dodging savvy—you can often tell when someone is dodging you, and there is a temptation to try to expose the perpetrator, to shame him, or to show you can't be fooled. This is a mistake. For everyone. Paranoia is an extremely unattractive quality and to be avoided at all costs. More important, there are certain things in society about which one is never supposed to speak. Dodging is one of these (that's why I had so much trouble getting people to cooperate in interviews). There are a few others—but I wouldn't dare list them here (See?).

You'll never know for sure whether or not someone is dodging you when she says she has the flu and hasn't left her house for two days. This is just one of life's little mysteries. Let it go. People are just doing what they have to do to get through the day. And if they've put some amount of effort into dodging you they should get credit for that anyway. I know that when I ask the waiter why there is no more cappuccino, I'd much rather he lie and tell me, "I'm so sorry, but the machine's on the blink," than "I'm sick of making cappuccino!"

7. CONFESSING TO THE DODGEE YOU HAVE DODGED HIM: Conversely, you must never, ever admit to someone that you have dodged him. Not talking about it is part of the reason dodging works. If everyone admitted their dodging practices to their friends and acquaintances, they would never be able to use those dodges on those friends and acquaintances. Secrecy is part of the system. To reveal your dodges would cause a breakdown of the intricate interactive infrastructure; people do not like it when you take away their social conventions. (In point of fact, I am breaking all kinds of rules in writing this book and shall probably be forced to move to another country right after its publication.)

THE IMPORTANCE OF BEING A REALLY GOOD LIAR

Let's take a quick look at what life would be like without lying.

You go down to the breakfast your wife is making for you. She asks you why you were tossing and turning in your sleep last night. You say it was probably because of the disturbing erotic dreams you kept having about her sister. Your wife inquires sarcastically if maybe you'd rather sleep with her sister from now on. You say that you think her sister is too stupid to have a conversation with, much less sleep with. Your wife picks up—and then throws—the remains of your breakfast, which you were still eating, into the sink and storms out of the house. When you get to work, your boss stops by your desk to ask you what you think of the new tie his daughter gave him for his birthday, which you confess you think looks like something bought at Kmart. Your boss raises an eyebrow and remarks that, as you won't be getting that raise after all, maybe you'd better get used to shopping at Kmart yourself. Next, a client phones and asks you to lunch. You do happen to be free for lunch, but you can't face the thought of having to listen to this particular client talk about his latest home repair project. You tell him you are not really in the mood to see him, that you would rather eat alone. Insulted, he cancels his account.

In another universe, everyone may tell the truth; there may be no need for lie detectors, policemen, or independent prosecutors. But not in this universe. People don't like to think about it, but all adult humans lie, whether it is a friendly fib ("You look lovely today!") or a cunning con ("I've got some etchings you must see. . . ."). The fact is that the world would be a truly terrible place if no one ever lied. The important thing, especially when you are dodging someone, is to be sure to lie well. Lying well means being convincing, and not getting caught. To help those of you who feel you are clumsy liars, here are a few simple rules to follow:

Stay as close to the truth as possible when lying. Most people know this rule instinctively. It is always easier to exaggerate the truth than to make up something completely false. If you are in a Junior League meeting that lasts until seven o'clock and you are trying to dodge something that starts at seven-thirty, you simply extend the meeting until eight (assuming, of course, that your dodge dupe is not a member of the Junior League). Not only is a half-truth easier to put over (you won't have to make up any of the specifics, such as where it is and what it is about), but it is easier to remember. Forgetting your lie after the fact is one of the main ways people get caught dodging.

If you're going to say it, sell it. You must act the part, whatever it is. You have to almost believe the lie yourself. It helps to use a bold lead-in, like "Can I be honest with you?" "I'll tell you the absolute truth," or even the well-worn "You'll never *believe* what happened to me. . . ."

Vary your alibis. Don't use the same excuse with the same person too many times. It lessens your credibility. I once had a business associate who had her office redecorated on what was a suspiciously numerous number of occasions. If you are a frequent dodger, make an effort to remember what lie you've told last, and don't be a repeat offender.

Tell your lie in an insular environment. If you are going to tell a whopper, make sure it is contained. If you lie to a person about spraining your ankle and that person is friends with your whole social circle, there WILL be a leak.

Once you start, go all the way. If you are challenged, stick to your lie no matter what. In fact, add to it—embellish it. The stronger your delivery, the better chance your story has of holding water. In any case, you really don't have anything to lose. They will never know for certain, and few things are more embarrassing than being caught in a lie. (**Note:** If you think there is a chance your lie is going to be positively disproved and your dodge might collapse, use the Double Dodge—see page 69).

Don't do it if you can't pull it off. If you tend to break out in a rash every time you tell a fib, then stick to the techniques in the book that are better suited to poor liars.

If you follow the basic precepts in this chapter and avoid committing one of the seven dodging sins, your conscience need never hurt you. On the other hand if you don't care anything about ethics, then you can forget all this talk about sins and guilt, and just get ready to dodge mercilessly.

CHAPTER 2

∾

Preemptive Strikes

Hello? Is this someone with good news or money?
No? Good-bye.

—JASON ROBARDS ANSWERING THE TELEPHONE IN
A THOUSAND CLOWNS

If you are the kind of person who always has an umbrella with him when it rains or who does her Christmas shopping before Thanksgiving, you may be already well acquainted with one of the best dodging methods within the realm of human interaction: the Preemptive Strike. A Preemptive Strike requires both foresight and planning, but it can stop your adversary dead in his tracks.

My friend Sandra told me about something that happened to her at work which inspired her to become proficient at this sort of nip-it-in-the-bud dodge. She was sitting at her desk one morning, blithely going about her business, when suddenly a woman she dislikes intensely (I'll call her Betty) appeared out of nowhere, sporting her date book and a toothy smile. For months, Betty had been pursuing an unwanted, out-of-office friendship with Sandra. Now, I should mention that besides being a truly obnoxious woman who wears enough perfume to camouflage a garbage truck and whose husband is what used to be rather delicately called a "lush," Betty happens to be the head of a department whose goodwill Sandra definitely needs. This makes dodging Betty's invitations a particularly trick proposition.

At the sight of Betty standing in front of her, Sandra cringed inwardly; she knew what was coming. Sure enough, Betty chirped, "So hey, you! What are you doing Friday night? Are you up for dinner at my place?"

Quickly Sandra ran through several possible excuses in her head and settled on the overused but still totally respectable "I'm so sorry, Betty, but I'm already having dinner with a friend Friday."

"Oh, that *is* too bad," Betty said. And then, before Sandra could congratulate herself on a clean getaway, Betty continued, "The thing is, I really want to have you over for dinner. What night *could* you make it? Since you seem to be the busy one, I'll just schedule it to suit you!" And so, much to Sandra's dismay, she ended up having to actually set a date for dinner at the home of Betty and the lush. She could only hope she would have the flu or a broken leg when the time came.

Alas, Sandra realized too late that she could have dealt with the Betty situation before it became critical. With a little creativity and forethought, she could have completely warded off the invitation. From that day on, Sandra swore she would never be vulnerable to this kind of foreseeable checkmate again.

Just as the best way to avoid disease is to practice preventive medicine, often the best way to avoid an undesirable encounter or an annoying request is to do your dodging before the ball is even thrown. Whenever you can anticipate a specific confrontation, you really should take the time and energy to employ one of the following social self-defense tactics. If you are proactive rather than reactive, there is a good chance you will be able to escape capture not only before the noose is tightened but before it is even placed around your neck.

HOW TO SHOOT BEFORE YOU SEE THE WHITES OF THEIR EYES

Though perhaps just a tiny bit presumptive in nature, this is a common preemptive technique that can serve as a good defense against many an "obligatory" social event or chore. To "shoot before you see the whites of their eyes," offer an irrefutable and long-standing excuse *well in advance of the request*. This makes your alibi seem less like a dodge and more like just a coincidental disclosure of personal information. For example, if— *before the above dinner-party denouement*—Sandra were to have mentioned to Betty in passing that she was sick to death of her boyfriend never letting her socialize with anybody but him (the big bully!) or that she had a diabetic cat at home that needed nursing, she could have begged off easily later, simply by reminding Betty of the previously professed problem. In fact, if your "advance fire" is heavy enough, the unwelcome request or invitation may never come at all. I know a man who casually mentions to the people he wishes to avoid socially that his wife has a grapefruit-size goiter on her neck. This is admittedly a risky lie (and I'd certainly love to know what his wife thinks about it), but the man in question assured me that it has saved him from numerous mind-numbing evenings.

An advertising account executive I know provided me with a perfect illustration of this particular forestalling maneuver. He told me that he recently acquired a new client who right away started calling him every other day with demands for progress reports and hand-holding. Of course, whatever it was the client wanted was invariably misplaced or unfinished—in other words, it existed somewhere in the vast universe known as the TO DO box. As soon as the account exec realized that constant hounding was going to be this pesky client's M.O.—and that the resulting daily dodging he was going to have to do would ultimately damage his relationship with the client—he put the following plan into action.

At nine o'clock one Monday morning, he called the client. "I've got great news," he told him. "The top brass have put your account on our A-one list. Basically what the restructuring means for us is that we've put together a bigger team to focus on your product—you know, more thorough market research, etcetera—and we should have a comprehensive picture for you by the end of the month. I think you'll be pleased." Just in case presenting the client with a date that was several weeks away wasn't enough to effectively ground him, the exec added, "Meanwhile, if you have anything for us, E-mail it to me and we'll get right on it." The two essential elements of this exchange are that the *exec* called the *client*—an action rather than a reaction—and that the exec offered unasked-for infor-mation rather than trying to respond to any specific demands of the client's. And, even though this client's bullshit detector was probably picking up some blips on the screen during this call, the exec did not receive another phone call from the client for about two weeks. During that time, the TO DO box universe had stopped expanding enough for the exec to deal with the account.

The key to this technique is timing. The information you reveal *must not* appear to be in direct response to whatever it is the person wants or needs from you. For instance, if customer X is waiting for an overdue check, be sure to let it slip to X in passing that "of course the check is not ready" *before* he calls you to demand said check. If you know your supervisor is going to ask you for your budget report, offer an explanation for why you have not finished the report *before* he asks you for it. While a preannounced kitchen renovation can stave off countless culinary chores, if someone asks you to cook some cupcakes for your child's school bake sale and you try to wing it on the spot with "Oh! I forgot to tell you, our stove blew up," you are going to end up with some major egg, sugar, and butter on your face.

THE CLOSED DOOR:
HOW TO BE UNEQUIVOCALLY UNAVAILABLE

Perhaps the smoothest type of preemptive dodging I have ever heard of came from an acquaintance of mine, Charlie. Charlie, who had been hanging out with a certain female friend of his for about a year, had come to feel that the friendship was too time-consuming for him; and much as he hated to admit it, the daily contact with the woman had gone from fun to tiresome. He knew he had been lazy in the way he had just let the friendship go on, and he felt too guilty to suddenly start rejecting her frequent invitations to movies and lunches. So one day he met her for coffee and told her he had just started a new project that was going to have him working day and night for four months. He provided details about the project, of course, merely exaggerating an actual work assignment. (Remember rule number one about lying: Always make your lie as close to the truth as possible.) He added that he was letting her know in advance so that she wouldn't take it personally that he wouldn't be able to see much of anyone during those four months—including her. He assured her that he was going to miss their fun times together but that the project was important and unavoidable.

This is a brilliant strategy for three reasons: (1) It nullifies the need for continual dodging. (2) It reconditions the woman; after four months of not seeing or speaking to Charlie that often she will hardly notice he is gone from her day-to-day life, having by then replaced him with other people or activities. In other words, Charlie will have broken the habit of the friendship. And (3) most important—and this is the crux of this technique—Charlie presented himself as being unavailable to *everyone*, not just to her. The conceit here is that your Door is Closed to the whole world, not just to one person.

There are, of course, much less mendacious forms of this dodge. When telemarketers call me, I tell them I never accept telephone solicitations. If an acquaintance asks me if I will take a look at his manuscript, I tell him I make it a rule never to read friends' manuscripts. If someone wants to borrow money from me, I tell her I never lend money—no matter what.

The Closed Door goes further than most other Preemptive Strikes. While it does not involve a complete burning of your bridges, it is more or less a permanent solution. (**Warning:** Don't forget to take into account the possible ramifications of your Closed Door message. If a friend wants to set you up on a date with an actor and you tell the friend you're very sorry but you never date actors, you'd better be sure the date's name isn't Brad Pitt.)

THE MACHINE GUN

The Machine Gun requires a bit of energy, but if you can pull it off it's a marvelous—if somewhat flashy—deflecting technique. Whenever this trick has been used on me I have admired its flamboyance even as I was being bamboozled by it. Here's how it works:

The minute you sense something disagreeable might be heading your way—for instance when you run into your Uncle Henry unexpectedly on the street and you can tell he is gearing up to ask you for the umpteenth time to quit trying to make it as a computer consultant and come in with him in his discount shoe business—just open your mouth and start firing questions, fast. The ploy works best if you pick a topic close to the subject's heart; in Uncle Henry's case, trout fishing. Before he has time to gather his wits about him—and as if it is something that has been plaguing your mind for some time—you blast him: "Oh! Henry! Listen! Somebody was asking me and I realized I didn't know—where do you get the best flies for trout fishing?" As soon as he begins to answer (and believe me, if it is one of his favorite subjects he *will* answer before he does anything else) you launch more questions at him, one after the other. Keep your finger on the trigger and don't let up for a second. "And I forget—where do you go for the best fishing?" "Now, how big are they running around this time of year?" "Wait—what was that great story you were telling me about last summer—you know, the one about the boat tipping over and the fish eating the sandwiches?" You will need to offset the inevitable inanity of some of your interrogatives with a high level of enthusiasm. The more interested you seem in Uncle Henry's favorite subject, the better the Machine Gun will work. Keep up the barrage until you can make a quick exit, leaving Uncle Henry standing dazed in the street with visions of trout fishing dancing in his head and the retail shoe world completely forgotten (at least for the time being).

You can use the Machine Gun to avoid just about any subject—from unwelcome questions about your recent job interview to potentially stormy political discussions. The essential component of this technique is not what you are dodging but how much ammunition you can come up with. Remember: Once you start bombarding your target, don't stop until you are ready to make a break for it.

RUSSIAN ROULETTE

In real-life Russian Roulette, a player spins the cylinder of a revolver loaded with one bullet, points the muzzle at his own head, and pulls the trigger. It is the ultimate gamble, an act of bravado that calls for nearly insane recklessness. While the dodging form of Russian Roulette will probably not kill you, it is not for the faint of heart. It can, however, be stunningly effective.

A freelance publicist named Jill provided me with a common and relatively mild variation of Russian Roulette. She has a colleague whom she has known a long time and who does a lot of favors for her in her business. Jill therefore feels obliged to return these favors by throwing the colleague a client or work assignment once in a while. The problem is that this particular favor-doing guy is a mediocre publicist—someone whom Jill is loath to recommend for fear of damaging her own reputation. So what Jill does is to wait until she knows the favor doer is totally booked up, and then she throws a minor client his way. Ninety-five percent of the time this works beautifully; the clueless colleague is forced to turn the work down and yet Jill gets the credit for a favor returned. In this way Jill succeeds in dodging her obligation to the colleague, while making it seem as if she is doing just the opposite.

There are an infinite number of circumstances tailor-made for Russian Roulette. Is there someone you feel you absolutely cannot get out of inviting to your dinner party? No problem. Just schedule the dinner for a time you are fairly sure the person cannot come. Do you need to return a disagreeable phone call? Easy: Return the call when you know the person you are calling can't come to the phone or can't talk long. (For tips about calling when you are sure of getting voice mail see Chapter 9.) Bothered by an overly obsequious salesman? Tell him you want to buy an item you know he doesn't have (and can't order). And yes, there is always a chance that the trick will backfire and you will end up with an unwanted dinner partner or an exhausting sales pitch. (After all, it's not called Russian Roulette for nothing.) But remember that the very believability of this technique lies in there being some amount of risk involved. You can't hurt someone's feelings by not inviting him to the party when you did invite him to the party. It's not your fault if he can't come, is it?

I have a friend named John who is well known for his love of fine restaurants. Regrettably, he is also well known for having no money. How does he reconcile these two diametrically opposed facts? He manages it this way: He goes out to dinner with a person or persons with whom he has never eaten before. They order multiple courses and fine wines. At the end of the meal John grandly offers to pay the entire bill, whipping out his American Express Card. Many restaurants, of course, don't accept American Express. The waiter invariably informs him of this fact. After a little indignation or embarrassment on John's part (whichever he is in the mood for that night), someone else at the table almost always steps in to save the day—often following John's lead by insisting on picking up the entire check. John then apologizes convincingly for not having any cash—though sometimes he will offer to pay at least part of the tip, with what is left in his wallet (usually a lonely twenty-dollar bill).

Although it can be a great dodge, playing Russian Roulette at this level is, without question, dangerous. Some restaurants *do* accept American Express, and in such cases John is pretty much stuck unless some genuinely gallant member of the party decides to fight him for the check. There is also the possibility that one of John's fellow diners will accuse him of being a deadbeat (though according to him this never happens, as most people are either too polite or too naive). John is what I call a dodging daredevil—he has the personality of a con artist and the morals of the original, pickpocketing Artful Dodger. I certainly would not recommend this check-dodging trick to most people, who would have neither the desire nor the chutzpah to pull it off. There are, however, plenty of other, more moderate ways to play this game—and win.

Russian Roulette is quite a commonly used strategy even though few people will ever admit to it. Without intending to propagate paranoia, I can assure you that this dodge has been used on everyone at some time or other. Just think about the times an invitation has arrived in your mailbox suspiciously close to the date of the event, or the times someone has called you back at 8:00 P.M. when you specifically told her you would be out all evening. Remember that time your sister offered you her crystal punch bowl right after you had given up hope of ever borrowing it and had gone out and bought one? You guessed it—Russian Roulette.

If you're good at bluffing in poker you should definitely consider making Russian Roulette part of your dodging repertoire. It is the most empowering of all the preemptive dodging methods; it's like staring your problems right in the face, sticking out your tongue, and saying, "Come and get me, I dare you!"

BULLETPROOF VESTING:
BASIC SAFETY TIPS

Since most of us are not psychics, we have no way to predict exactly what is going to be thrown at us. Nine times out of ten we end up saying yes to things merely because we can't come up with the right way to say no to something on the spot. After all, it can be difficult not to fold under pressure when your grandmother suddenly springs it on you that she is coming to inspect your new apartment—the day after you've thrown a wild toga party—or when the grizzled, tattooed man you see on the bus every morning suddenly asks for your phone number.

Often you are not even sure you will need to dodge. When a friend of a friend calls you out of the blue to take you out to dinner or you get invited to a large party of people you won't know, it's hard to tell whether it will be a nightmare experience or a Kodak moment. Now, as Miss Mingle I firmly believe you must *never* forgo an unknown social event, as life's most pleasant surprises are usually found in unfamiliar arenas. But that doesn't mean you should face these events without protection. Like a secret agent donning his bulletproof vest before entering a dark alley, a truly artful dodger knows that the best defense against the unexpected is to be prepared. So here are a few basic safety procedures that can save your life—or at least your evening.

DO RECONNAISSANCE: Scope out the territory. Case the joint. If it's a party, find out who is going to be there before agreeing to attend. If it's a blind date, find out as much as possible about the date. If it's your wife's family reunion, make an effort to find out where the social sinkholes are before you go, and which of the relatives is likely to try to sell you insurance or a used car. If it's a sales conference, try to find out who else is staying in the same hotel you are—so you'll know if you'll need to put out your

Do Not Disturb sign. If it's an interview or an audition, try to find out beforehand what materials they need to see and what they might ask you. Sometimes, of course, this type of pre-information is not available. But if you can get the lay of the land before you go, it will greatly lessen your chances of needing to dodge.

STAY AWAY FROM LOBSTER TRAPS: Before you attend a gathering of any kind, make sure you know where the exit is. I mean this literally as well as figuratively. Like the cleverly constructed lobster trap, which has a cone-shaped entrance of netting so that the unsuspecting lobster can easily get in but not out, some events are impossible to escape from once you are there. My old high school friend Gretchen told me a horror story about going on a four-hour-long singles' cruise around Manhattan, where she didn't know a soul. (I think I spilled my drink when she told me this, so shocked was I that a seemingly intelligent woman would actually get on a boat, with no way off of it, to ride around with complete strangers for that long.) Twenty minutes after the cruise began Gretchen realized that: (1) she had nothing in common with any of the people on board, (2) she was not at all prepared to fend off constant requests for her phone number, and (3) she was prone to seasickness. Gretchen admitted to me that at various points throughout the evening she seriously considered jumping off and swimming to shore.

The closest I have come to having this kind of experience was at a buffet dinner with sailboat fanatics years ago in suburban Chicago. I was stuck in the middle of what seemed like no-where—with no way to get home, as my date had driven me and didn't want to leave. Everyone was playing a special game of sailing charades that went on for hours, to which the answers were things like "the wind." (Strangers and boats don't go well together. Unless, of course, you have your own cabin.) I realized later I shouldn't have gone to this dinner without an escape plan.

You should also be careful about accepting overnight (or longer) invitations to the homes of people you don't know very well. It's a very sticky business indeed to get up and leave in the middle of a weekend in the Catskills. Similarly, think twice before inviting someone you don't know well to stay in *your* home. Once I offered my spare room to a couple—cousins of a friend of mine. "Any cousins of Clayton's are cousins of mine!" I remember telling them gaily on the phone. What I didn't tell them was that they were not expected to yell and curse at each other the whole time they were here. Which they did. My southern hospitality went south after that and stayed there, but I learned a valuable lesson: Never commit to something unknown when there is no way out.

TAKE A LIFE RAFT ALONG: When entering an unknown social or business sphere, always tell whoever it is that you have a time limit. ("I'd love to come but I have to get to my piano lesson at four P.M.") This safety device will allow you to accept invitations and experiences that you might be too afraid to otherwise. If the experience turns out to be wonderful, you can always change your mind and pretend to cancel whatever it is, should you so desire ("Oh, the heck with my piano lesson! I haven't practiced this week anyway!"). In other words, you don't have to actually inflate the life raft. It's really just for stormy weather. This is an especially good strategy for first dates or first meetings of any kind. One man I interviewed told me he used this device religiously during the three years he lived in Europe. Because of his being an American in Vienna, other Americans would frequently call him up when they were visiting, having gotten his number from an acquaintance back in the States. He would usually accept invitations to socialize with these veritable strangers, but he always made it clear he had a limited time slot available—an hour or an hour and a half.

DEVELOP AN EARLY WARNING SYSTEM: I know two women who are partners in an art gallery. Naturally they are obliged to do a lot of schmoozing with people in the art business and with potential buyers. Over the years they have developed a great cooperative mingling system, which they call "Buddies in the Foxhole." Part of this system consists of a code to warn each other when someone difficult or unpleasant is on the mingling horizon. For example, when one of them sees a person approaching who is liable to monopolize the conversation and will be hard to get away from, one of them will drop the appropriate code word into the conversation (they wouldn't even tell me the code word—it's secret), and then they both scatter if they can.

CARRY VERBAL HAND GRENADES: Never face difficult or uncharted social battlefields without at least one excuse in your pocket. For instance, if you are going to a bar, be sure to have at least one excuse handy for using on undesirable persons asking to buy you a drink. Don't wait until the lech is leering at you so disgustingly and intensely that you can't think of anything but "Keep your hands off of me, you cad." Instead, have three lines ready: "I never accept drinks from men I don't intend to talk to," or "My drinks are already paid for," or even "Oh thanks! Drinking helps my yeast infection!" One of my friends, a freelance writer who is a great dodger, told me he never answers his phone without having an ironclad, unverifiable excuse on the tip of his tongue—one for dodging invitations and another one for dodging work demands.

AVOID MINEFIELDS: Be aware of your surroundings, and *think before you speak*. We hear this cliché so much while we are growing up that it should be second nature by the time we are adults, but it isn't. You can avoid having to dodge about 50 percent of the time if you remember this axiom. Always be aware of who is within earshot. Don't talk about social events in front of someone you don't want to invite. Don't talk about favors you did for someone else in front of someone who could possibly ask you the same favor. When someone asks you what you are doing tomorrow night, never answer "Nothing," always say, "I'll have to check my calendar." When in doubt, say "I'm not sure." If you don't get yourself into things, you won't have to get yourself out of them.

Whether you are cave diving or lunching with business associates, having the proper protective gear can give you the confidence to get out there and explore new territory. And although you will probably not have the energy or the inclination to be thinking ahead all the time, there is no question that preemptive strategies can help you ward off many of life's minor problems. And if they don't, you can always. . . . Duck—and Cover.

CHAPTER 3

❦

The Duck and Cover

When ideas fail, words come in very handy.
—GOETHE

The Duck and Cover is by far the world's most common escape maneuver. An evolutionary descendant of primitive man's fear/response instinct, the Duck and Cover (otherwise known as the Crouch and Run) is the way most of us deal with trouble when we are caught off guard. Just as Cro-Magnon man would have dodged a spear and run back into his cave, so now do we sidestep a dangerous question and head for the executive washroom. If you read no further in this book but can become an expert at the Duck and Cover, you will be able to handle much of whatever the fates hurl at you.

This simple technique requires no advance preparation, but you need a strong sense of survival and a bit of practice to get really good at it. Almost everyone knows the fundamentals of the Duck and Cover. However, there are things you can do to make the performance of it more seamless—as well as variations you can add to make it more convincing.

STEP ONE: THE DUCK

Imagine you are lying on your couch watching TV. The phone rings. Because you are in a *Jeopardy/Simpsons*-induced trance you pick it up without thinking twice.

The nightmare begins; it's your mother-in-law. "So what's going on? You haven't left the house yet?" booms her voice into your ear. Heart pounding, you suddenly remember you were supposed to be having dinner at her place (your wife is out of town). Not only are you in your underwear and socks at the moment but also going to your mother-in-law's house for dinner is the last thing you want to do right now—especially since you have just called out for pizza.

The goal of step one is to delay, to freeze the action until you can find your script. You need a little time to gather your wits about you and decide what to do. The most important thing to remember: Never show dismay or fear of any kind. In fact, one of the most helpful skills for you to acquire is the ability to project an unruffled pre-Duck air; you are going to fare a lot better if you can throw the object of your dodge off the scent with an enthusiastic—even joyous—greeting ("Oh HI, MOM!" or "Hello! Glad to hear your voice!"). This is especially important for face-to-face encounters, where body language is half the battle. A positive stance will relax the object of your Duck and will ultimately make your Cover more credible. Then go right into the Duck itself:

"Listen Ma? I'm right in the middle of a household emergency—I'll call you back in two minutes." Now—and this is *crucial*—hang up immediately. Don't allow any space for further conversation. You need time to think up a good excuse for not showing up to dinner (and to decide conclusively that you don't want to go). Always try to Duck in as vague a manner as possible, so that after your brain starts functioning at normal adrenaline levels you will have more leeway in concocting an excuse.

The best delaying strategies are ones in which the object of your ducking is forced to go away while you take time to construct your Cover. Second best are ones that allow you to put the person on hold; the least desirable Ducks (but ones that sometimes can't be helped) are those where the person is standing there in front of you while you are scrambling for cover. While the Duck and Cover is ideal for handling telephone surprises, it can also be performed in face-to-face situations. If the object of your dodge *should* happen to be physically present, you use your Duck to remove yourself from him, altogether or at least for a few minutes. (If you are on the street, you can run off to catch a bus; if you are in a room together, go make a phone call, or get a cup of coffee.) For more about face-to-face escape maneuvers, see Chapter 10.

Sample Ducking Lines

Keep in mind that the lines below are designed to deliver you only temporarily from your difficulty. You must be prepared to present your Cover shortly thereafter. One line may afford you a delay of only a minute or two; another might provide you with a reprieve of several days. (**Note:** These lines are offered mostly for inspiration. You should adapt them to fit the circumstances.)

"Let me look around for that. . . ."

"Hi—oh . . . wait . . . sorry-I'll-have-to-call-you-back!"

"Oh . . . right . . . yes we will have to talk about that."

"Wait, let me switch to a better phone."

"I can't hear a thing right now, I just got off the plane."

"You've been on my mind all day—but let me call you back."

"Someone is in my office right now."

"I just got out of the shower and I'm dripping wet."

"Let me just finish writing down my thought."

"Right now I've got glue [ink/paint/grease/flour] on my hands."

"There is something on the stove that's boiling over."

"Oh no! The cat—wait—Snowball! Bad cat! Call-you-back-bye."

"I've got a kid here running around with no diaper on."

"Wait—I just remembered something. I'll call you back."

"I was just walking out the door."

"I am so unbelievably late at the moment . . . I've got to dash."

"I've *got* to find the bathroom *right* now, I'll talk to you later."

"I'm going to find my seat but I'll see you at halftime."

"Wait . . . what time is it? Darn, got to feed the meter."

"Hold that thought. . . ."

STEP TWO: THE COVER

Okay. You've succeeded in making life stand still for a moment. You are safe for the time being, so take a deep breath and concentrate. You've got to come up with a Cover, a compelling excuse that will get you out of whatever it is without anyone's being upset with you.

Let's say you used the above "household emergency" Duck. There are an infinite number of Cover options (the bathroom pipe just burst, you didn't realize fixing the heater would take you all day, the vacuum cleaner exploded, the ceiling fell down, etc.). The question is: Which one will seem the most plausible to your dodgee? It has to (1) sound serious enough to have been the cause of your foul-up, (2) be something that could actually happen to you, and (3) be a continuation or extension of whatever you alluded to in your initial ducking line.

Before committing to a Cover, be sure to consider carefully who it is you are going to tell this lie (or half lie) to and exactly what kind of access the person has to your life. In other words, how easy will it be for her to disprove your lie later? If you tell your mother-in-law the sink flooded, totally swamping the kitchen (which you are now cleaning up), she'll probably never be the wiser; but if you tell her the drapes in the den caught fire, you'll have to go shopping for new drapes first thing in the morning. Also don't forget principle number one: Always stay as close to the truth as possible. It's no good telling "Ma" that you had to take the dog to the emergency room if later when she asks you how Patches is you are going to look at her blankly and say, "Fine, why?" It's hard enough to remember your real life; you don't want to have to remember a lot of details from a made-up one. This is why it's always safer if you can create your Cover out of something that is just urgent enough to cause the cancellation of an evening, but not life-altering. That way no one will doubt you when, two weeks later, you have no immediate recollection of the event.

One last thing: Don't forget to cover any "tracks" you may have made during your Duck; if there were people laughing and clapping in the background when you were supposed to be home alone, incorporate this evidence into your Cover story.

("The whole darn neighborhood was over here to see why there was smoke coming out of my windows!")

(**Note:** Although you can use the excuses in Chapter 5 to give you ideas for your Cover, Cover excuses will differ somewhat—due to the nature of the situations that spawn them. The Duck and Cover is almost solely for fending off surprise attacks; therefore the Cover excuse has to reflect your behavior at the time of the attack.)

HOT POTATO: PASSING THE BUCK

Sometimes the easiest way to cope with an incoming problem is with a pass. Passing the buck is often considered the coward's way out, but if you are about to get badly burned and there is someone handy to pass to, I say pass! (Of course, the thing itself has to be passable; in the case of the mother-in-law and the dinner, there would be no way to pass the buck.) Don't feel too bad: If you do choose to pass, chances are the person you passed to will lob one over in your corner tomorrow and then you can both have a good laugh about it. Anyway, what is a major hot potato to you might be as cool as a cucumber to someone else who is not having your kind of day. The person you pass to might be better equipped to deal with whatever it is. She might even be a better dodger. Or perhaps she has never been in trouble with this particular dodgee before so you know whatever the fallout is, it won't hurt her as much as it would hurt you. Or maybe you just don't care. Let her pass to someone else if she can. After all, all's fair in love and dodging. There are simply times you have to admit you are not going to be able come up with a good Cover and you have no other choice. Then your Duck and Cover becomes the Duck and Pass.

Sample Duck and Pass Scenario

The Problem: "Hello, Dr. Smith? I'm a friend of your sister. She told me you wouldn't mind giving me an interview about your work in the field of sports medicine. It's for the neighborhood paper—and I'm afraid the deadline's today. But your sister assured me you wouldn't mind helping me out. So if you wouldn't mind giving me about twenty minutes of your time?"

The Duck: "Anything for a friend of my sister . . . but can you hold on while I get rid of the person on the other line?"

The Pass: "Listen, I'd be happy to help out but I really don't know as much about this as my colleague Susie Jones. She's the one to talk to. Tell her I told you she was the best in the field. Here's her number. . . ."

(**Warning:** You must be certain that the person you pass to is not going to toss the potato in question right back in *your* lap. The longer it's been in the air, the hotter that potato is going to get. If it comes back to you it's likely to burn the skin off your fingers.)

THE LAME DUCK OR
DON'T LET THIS HAPPEN TO YOU

John Johnson was under a lot of pressure at work. It was his company's busy season, and he had just arrived back from his vacation to discover that his secretary had quit without notice. Consequently, he was having to field his own calls, something he was not used to doing. By mid-morning he was completely frazzled. He had just knocked the overflowing In Box onto the floor—scattering the papers like confetti—when the phone rang. It was one of his biggest purchasers, wanting prices from him—A.S.A.P.

"Can you hold on a sec?" John said as cheerfully as he could, and then he put the pushy purchaser on hold. He began to curse to himself as he searched through the chaos of papers around him, "That goddamn moron . . . he has to call me with this now? Why can't he wait for me to call him with the friggin' figures. . . ." Finally he found what he needed and got back on the phone, first taking a deep breath. "Okeydoke," he said to the buyer, "I've got that right here. Should I read it to you or shall I fax it?" There was an odd silence on the other end of the line and then the purchaser replied in icy tones, "Oh no. I wouldn't want you to have to deal with a moron like me, John. I think I'll just work things out with your superior from now on." John realized with horror that he had pushed the wrong button and failed to put the buyer on hold!

The Lame Duck is not something you ever want to experience. It may happen if you are careless during the process of ducking. Make sure you've really put the person on hold. Be certain not to be overheard—whether you are at a party or on the other side of a thinner-than-you-thought door. Also be careful not to make the mistake of using the same ducking line on one person three times in a row—especially if it is something very specific like "spilling coffee" right after you pick up the phone. ("Hey listen, Bub. Nobody spills that much coffee!") Unfortunately, if you make this kind of mistake when you are ducking your boss or your most important client, you are going to end up not just a Lame Duck but a Dead Duck.

CHAPTER 4

∞

The Absentminded Professor

The first duty in life is to be as artificial as possible.
What the second duty is no one has yet discovered.
—OSCAR WILDE

It's an important club meeting. You R.S.V.P.'ed weeks ago that you'd be there. You know it's going to cost you big time if you go; not only are they sure to ask you to chair a subcommittee but also you know that someone is bound to hit you up for money. The kicker is that someone has just given you great tickets to a baseball game, and the thought of sitting in a meeting on a beautiful summer evening has now gone from unappetizing to unacceptable.

Unfortunately, several people in the club have seen you at work during the day—so it would be extremely difficult to plead illness or a family emergency. After considering all your viable options, you conclude that there's really only one thing left for you to do. *This is a job for the Absentminded Professor!*

THE BEAUTY OF SELF-EFFACEMENT

Think Columbo. Think Jerry Lewis. Think Mr. Magoo and Lucy Ricardo. Forget about your pride, your dignity, your ego, and your id. For this dodge, you need people to feel sorry for you. In fact, they are going to feel so sorry for you that they will not be angry at or disappointed in you. Why? Because you are going to be too angry at and disappointed in yourself. You are going to be so busy beating yourself up that no one else will have time to take a swing at you. Moreover, you are going to seem too addle-brained for them to feel anything but pity for you. Pity, which is not usually an emotion we like to elicit from anyone, is your number one objective in the Absentminded Professor.

This truly artful artifice is created by combining an "I forgot" excuse with a well-acted, self-effacing apology. The beauty of the self-effacing apology is that you gain the sympathy of the person you are dodging by showing him your "blunder" is making *you* suffer. Often this dodge works so well that the person ends up trying to make *you* feel better, even though you are the one who let *him* down.

Your apology, mind you, must be good. You've got to sound as if you really mean it. If you don't feel sorry at all, resort to the traditional actor's method: Try to recall a time in your life when you *did* feel sorry and use that memory to project a convincing amount of repentance in the here and now. (Love might mean never having to say you're sorry but the Absentminded Professor means you have to say it all the time.) Obviously, this technique is not suitable for people with an overabundance of pride.

GUIDELINES FOR EFFECTIVE
ABSENTMINDEDNESS

Let's say you spent the evening at the baseball park instead of at the meeting. It's now the next day—time to don your Absentminded Professor camouflage for your postmeeting dodge. When you call up the chairman of the meeting (or whoever is the head of the Members' Groveling Department) try to get a sort of grandfatherly, Ronald Reagan thing happening in your voice (yes, even if you are female): "Fred? [chuckle] It's me . . . the sharpest tack in the box. . . . I can't apologize enough for missing that meeting. I wish I had a good excuse, but the truth is that I just totally forgot all about it! [more chuckling] I was watching the ten o'clock news when suddenly I remembered about the darn thing. . . . I can't believe it, I had it written down and everything. Do you think I need to get some of that new memory medication?"

The Absentminded Professor can serve as an alter ego—a kind of anti-superhero whose special power is superstupidity—whom you can call upon to help you out of emergencies. It is best suited for those times when you have failed to show up for an appointment or social event, or when you have failed to accomplish a task you were supposed to have done. It is not, I repeat *not*, to be used to justify standing someone up (see the Seven Dodging Sins, page 11). And it is not going to work in situations where you were reminded about an event an hour beforehand—unless you are ready to transmute your Absentminded Professor act into a Head Trauma/Temporary Amnesia act. And that only works on soap operas.

Here are other examples of the Absentminded Professor hard at work:

BEFORE AN EVENT: "Listen, I know I told you I was coming tonight but when I finally dug my calendar out from under the pile of unread magazines and papers, I found that I had made a previous engagement I forgot all about. . . . I know, I *know* . . . I need a personal assistant—or maybe a keeper!"

DURING AN EVENT: "Oh my god! I just remembered I am supposed to be at my nephew's soccer game! I am going to get the bad aunt of the year award. This is the third time. . . . I am such a space cadet, I am so sorry, I have to run. . . ."

AFTER MISSING AN EVENT: "You should not even have to *have* a friend like me. I wrote it in my calendar but like the true Alzheimer's case I am, I wrote it in the wrong month! Like, do I even *know* what month it is? Isn't that one of the questions they ask you to tell if you are insane or not?"

"I can't believe it. I fell asleep and just woke up a little while ago."

ABOUT SOMETHING YOU DIDN'T DO: "I totally forgot I was supposed to call you! I am such an idiot."

"I am such a dunderhead, I completely forgot to write the check until this morning! I'm lucky I haven't walked in front of a bus, I swear."

"I was walking down the street yesterday and suddenly I stopped and yelled out loud—really, people turned around and stared—because I realized I had forgotten all about the letter I was supposed to give you last week! How is this possible? Do I seem old to you? I think I am losing it."

WHEN YOU WANT TO DITCH SOMEONE: "Well we are all supposed to meet at this restaurant later but I can't tell you exactly where the restaurant is. I can probably find it myself if I wander around enough—I mean, I've been there several times—but I can never remember anything anymore. All I know is it's Italian and it's somewhere on the West Side between Seventy-second and Eighty-sixth."

Of course, you have to be prudent about how much you portray this pathetic character. You don't want to get a reputation for being a *complete* idiot, and if you play the Absentminded Professor too much at work you could find yourself suddenly facing early retirement. But as an occasional device—when you really need it—this ploy can work like a dream (or should I say like a delusion).

OFFERS OF PENANCE

The Absentminded Professor is one of the few dodging techniques that require you to openly admit that you are at fault. This can cause unforeseen repercussions. Sometimes you will learn after the fact that nobody else showed up at the meeting either; if so, you will feel the need to do a little more smoothing over—a little guilt cleanup. You might simply have misjudged how peeved the other person was going to be—or how well you were going to be able to convince the person of your absentmindedness. In any case, it is usually not a bad idea to top off this dodge with an offer of penance.

You can offer a return engagement ("Let me make it up to you. I'll take you to lunch—if I can remember how to get to the restaurant—ha-ha"), a makeup chore ("How about if I take your carpool mornings for two weeks as restitution—that is, if you trust me to drive your kids"), or even a forgive-me gift ("Please accept this pen as an apology and a symbol that I promise to write things down from now on"). When all else fails, money can be the ultimate fixer-upper ("I feel like a cad for missing the fund-raiser but please accept the enclosed check. Hope this helps").

THE DEAF AND DUMB DODGE

The Deaf and Dumb Dodge is a close cousin of the Absentminded Professor and can serve you well in certain types of emergencies. It also can be amazingly effortless. My friend Chiva reminded me about this tactic when she was telling me about a near miss she had while attending a memorial service. The nature of the occasion had put her a bit off her game (she is British and tends to say things like that), which is why she was not paying too much attention when a certain nonfriend of hers asked her what she was doing on Sunday. "Me?" she said, "Oh, nothing." She realized her mistake immediately, and sure enough, the nonfriend continued with, "Oh great! I'm having a picnic, and Joe's driving out so you can get a ride with him . . . I'll let him know you'll need a ride. . . ." She kept talking. Now, luckily for Chiva there were other people standing in the same circle, people who were also invited to the picnic. So what did Chiva do? Absolutely nothing. She kept a vague, slight smile on her face all the time the nonfriend was talking about the picnic, but she never responded, never nodded, never even inclined her head to any of the picnic details. Sunday came and went without any disturbance in Chiva's day. When the nonfriend saw her about a week later and asked her where she had been on Sunday, Chiva told her she had been so distracted at the service that the invitation had never really registered.

The trick to the Deaf and Dumb Dodge is passivity. You've got to become a rock and let the requests flow over you like rushing water. The words—like the water—are there, but they don't move you. This technique is useful if you are not great at lying, because basically all that is required is that you keep your mouth shut.

There is also a garden variety of the Deaf and Dumb Dodge that I call simply the Deaf Dodge. It is a more subtle maneuver, one that people use all the time without thinking much about it. Here's an example: One day I was walking down the street with a new acquaintance. We were talking about careers and life, but secretly I was trying to find out how old he was. He mentioned that he had come to Manhattan to start his business in the 1980s.

"So how old were you when you moved here?" I slyly asked him. But my cleverness proved less than his. "When did I come?" he replied, "in 1985." He pretended to mishear what I said, yet answered the gist of my question. For me to have pressed him further would have been too obvious. (Score one for him.)

This kind of evasion is seen a lot in E-mail exchanges and is perfect for dodging undesirable topics and requests. It's a marvelous sidestepping tool when you are asked to offer an opinion or decision on something that—for one reason or another—you are loath to give. Politicians use this kind of circumvention every day, with a frequency that is not recommended for the layperson. But as an occasional ploy, it's considered a completely conventional conversational practice.

CHAPTER 5

Excuses, Excuses

I'd love to kiss you, but I just washed my hair.
—BETTE DAVIS IN
THE CABIN IN THE COTTON

Everyone knows that in order to be an artful dodger you must have a myriad of excuses ready at all times. The reason you need so many is that you need to be able to vary them. Varying your excuses is essential to your long-term credibility; if every time you turn down an invitation you have a cold and every time you don't want to talk about the budget you've got a headache, you may as well give up and tell the truth. (And *nobody* wants that.)

Authentic-sounding excuses are vital to day-to-day life. Like good salesmanship, the ability to excuse yourself well makes life more palatable. It allows others to hold on to the illusion that everything is okay. (You *don't* dislike them; you *didn't* find something better to do; you *aren't* a terrible assistant; you are *not* letting them down—you just have a migraine!) Frankly, people who dodge a commitment without offering a well-crafted excuse make me angry. It shows a lack of respect for the other person not to put some energy into a good excuse. An unadorned "Sorry, I can't come after all," when there is a place set for you at the table and a quail in the oven with your name on it is not a proper refusal. It shows bad manners and a carelessness about the feelings of others. In fact, in my opinion, to say no to someone without using an excuse—if that someone has good reason to expect something of you—is the height of narcissism. Even if you are someone with virtually no imagination, you can at least manage to produce one of the classic excuses below. (**Reminder:** When deciding upon and offering up your excuse, please keep in mind the Six Principles of Prevarication, page 17.)

THE CLASSICS:
PROS AND CONS OF THE MOST COMMON EXCUSES

Clichés become clichés because they are frequently true. Likewise, the classic excuses can be the most effective ones because they are so often things that really happen. They are also hard to refute. However, because a classic line can seem so generic, whenever you use one you've got to wipe the dust off of it a bit. In other words, you can't say "I don't have a thing to wear" (unless you are being droll) but you *can* say "I was all set to come when I realized all my good dresses were at the cleaners and it was too late to get them." You've got to add a twist—some personal details—to the classic dodging lines.

Let's look at the pros and cons of some traditional excuses:

Being Sick

Pros: As excuses go, sickness is one of the best. Society has been calling in sick for centuries. Whether it is in the form of a plain old headache or the more trendy sinus infection, feigning illness can provide you with many an escape. A simple "I'm so sorry, I haven't had any sleep," will work as a minor dodge; more serious problems may necessitate something like "I should never have come out tonight with this herniated disk—I'm not myself at all." Or even "That wasn't me talking, that was my ulcer. . . . Forgive me, I'm in so much pain I don't know what I'm doing." Acceptable malingerer's excuses include flu, cold, food poisoning (a favorite among artful dodgers because it is not contagious and relatively short-lived), migraine, P.M.S., gum surgery, pulled muscle, back problems, poison ivy, and jet lag. The Sick Excuse is multipurpose; it can explain everything from canceling a get-together to performing poorly on the job.

Cons: The problem with the Sick Excuse is that it is so overused that it is always suspect, which was the reason for requiring the proverbial "note from a doctor." Many dodgers will try to spice up their "call-in" with the handkerchief over the receiver trick (to sound stuffed up) or coughing in between phrases, but if this doesn't come off well it can cause a lot of eye rolling on the other end of the phone. Then of course you have to be sure to *stay* in your Camille role, and not get caught playing tennis when you are supposed to be in bed with a fever. If you happen to tell someone you are suffering from something like Lyme disease, you've got a long acting job ahead of you. Not only that, but if you play sick too much you can get a reputation as a hypochondriac. You might be considered contagious, weakly, or undependable. Also never forget that playing sick can backfire: Use the "flu" to evade work and you might not get invited to that screening you wanted to go to. And there is always the danger that if you keep telling people you are sick your body could start to believe what you are saying.

The Kid Excuse

Pros: This may be the most effective excuse in existence. People who have children can use them to get out of almost anything anytime. (I've often thought about having a few just so I could get out of stuff.) The needs of children are always sacrosanct; whether you say your child is sick, cranky, mopey, or nervous; that you couldn't get a babysitter or that he just needs to be driven somewhere, people will accept it. Unlike more of the other classic excuses, this one is rooted in a sense of duty, rather than in the usual combination of powerlessness and discomfort.

Cons: The only potential downside of this alibi is that if you use it a lot people may start to think you have no life beyond the kids. And once you use it a couple of times with the same person, he might cross you off his invitation list and stop calling you for fear of bothering you. In fact, an overworking of the Kid Excuse could bring an undesired, permanent end to your need for dodging altogether.

Stuck in Traffic

Pros: Often employed by people who are late (usually for work), the Stuck in Traffic Excuse is so old it probably got started back in horse and buggy days ("Finally I had to just get out of the carriage and walk!"). It encompasses not being able to get a taxi, your car breaking down, subway or train malfunctions, accidents on highways, and the generally abhorred, run-of-the-mill rush-hour traffic jam. The most attractive thing about this excuse is its absolute incontestability.

Cons: Unfortunately, *because* of its incontestability, people whom you are dodging with this excuse can be very suspicious. Better make your in-transit horror story good—and use it sparingly.

The Check Is in the Mail

Pros: This is popular because here you are not explaining why something has not been done but instead claiming that it has. This makes it fairly shame-free as excuses go. Variations on this theme include "I sent the package out yesterday," "The messenger just picked it up and is on his way over," and "I can't believe you didn't get that; I sent it a week ago—I'll check on it right now."

Cons: This is really only a delaying tactic, a semi-dodge. The person either believes you or he doesn't; but in either case he suspends judgment only for three or four days. And if you can't get whatever it is to him within a reasonable time period, you are going to lose face, and maybe a customer.

Pros: This excuse is ideal when you have forgotten to call someone, or have failed to take care of something in a timely fashion. It's *essential* to add details to this one; without them it's not really an excuse at all. "I lost my address book," works best (but only once every year or so, please); "I lost the number in the move," and "I lost it while I was traveling" are also acceptable. You might prefer the Absentminded Professor style of this excuse: "I think it's buried somewhere under the pile of papers in my office!" Many people like to use the "lost number" excuse because while it's not a particularly strong dodge, it takes very little imagination and even less energy to present.

Cons: Most of us don't really take well to hearing someone has lost our number—no matter what the circumstances. Especially offensive is the "I threw it out by mistake" version of this excuse. The victims of this dodge feel that in some way you are—consciously or subconsciously—throwing *them* out (although if it is discarded by your spouse, your child, your assistant, or the maid, it is passable). In any case, if you hide behind this "lost number" too often people will begin to suspect you are an imbecile or a liar—or both.

The Computer Is Down

Pros: Claiming your computer is "down" is perfectly fine, but since it by now has become a cliché, better forms of this excuse are: "They installed a new program on all the computers in the office and we haven't quite worked all the bugs out," or "We had a major computer virus" (which also elicits sympathy).

Blaming technology (see also Chapter 9) is an almost flawless excuse choice; almost everyone has daily frustrations with computers. This makes this relatively new classic excuse the most unimpeachable of them all.

Cons: There is only one real danger in using this excuse. If you are using it with someone in business who needs to be able to count on the effectiveness of your technology, it's going to make you look bad. In other words, if you work at IBM, your computers can never be "down."

Working Late

Pros: It's hard to argue with your need to earn a living, and the image of you slaving away at your desk is definitely preferable to one of you dancing away at someone else's party. But whether you claim your boss tossed something unexpected your way or you have a client coming in from out of town, please avoid the almost comically common pitfall—telling someone you are at the office when they could easily call and find out you left hours ago.

Cons: This classic is so overused that it is sometimes not very effective. Ironically, even though it is so often not a fib, the I-had-to-work-late defense is possibly the most distrusted one in the book. It is therefore best to use this excuse only when you can't come up with anything else. When you do employ it, be sure to sound appropriately miserable about your plight. "I hate my life" is always a nice touch here.

THE TERRIBLE HORRIBLE VERY BAD DAY

One of my favorite movie scenes is in *Crimes of the Heart*, when Jessica Lange asks Sissy Spacek to explain why she was trying to kill herself and Spacek replies, "I was just havin' a *real bad* day."

Everyone knows what it feels like to have a bad day (although usually not bad enough to want to end it all). The great thing about selling people this bill of goods is that even if they don't completely buy it, they are duty bound by the rules of politeness to listen to your complaints and make some sympathetic noises. When you hit them with your frantic, "I am *so* sorry I didn't get that extremely important report done, and now you have to go to the sales conference empty-handed, but I am having the absolute *worst* day of my life," it will at least slow them down if not stop them from focusing on the problem at hand.

A lot of people like to use this subterfuge because of how easily it flows off the tongue when you are stressed out. After all, you are probably *not* having a great day, as you are having to dodge someone. Now all you have to do is pick two or three other terrible things that could very well have happened to you—you were splashed by a taxi, had your wallet stolen, discovered the man you are dating is a married ax murderer—and recount the fictitious horror story of your day. (There are some days you will have to exaggerate only a little bit!) Your freshly made error or omission will then become just another part of this "bad day," just a small piece of a run of bad luck, with which everyone can empathize.

Here are some suggested mishaps and misfortunes from which to create your own, very special bad day:

Got yelled at by the boss/had fight with spouse/busted high heel/got stood up/were notified you are being audited by IRS/found out you need disgusting dental procedure/were fired from a job/lost your keys/saw old boyfriend with new wife/ pigeon went to bathroom on your head/bought something expensive that doesn't work/got roped into weekend with in-laws/found out you couldn't have children/broke a nail/bounced a check/got mugged/therapist made a pass at you/got obscene phone call/your pet hamster died/girlfriend dumped you/lost the rent money in a poker game/forgot your best friend's birthday/lost your best friend/got bit by neighbor's dog/your dog bit neighbor/son smashed your car/daughter flunked English/grandson arrested/basement flooded/roof leaking/children's nanny quit/dyed your hair wrong color/ houseguest broke family heirloom/found cockroach in food/ studied wrong textbook for final exam/flew to Texas for meeting that was canceled/dropped heavy object on recently healed foot/lost last quarter in faulty vending machine/raw sewage leak in apartment/landlord is trippling your rent/ tripped over crack in sidewalk and skinned everything so now pantyhose are caked with blood.

Mix and match, throw in a touch of Method acting, and you are on your way.

Thank god for the New Age. Not only has it given us materialistic westerners meditation techniques, psychic readings, and polarity therapy but it has provided us with one of the most irrefutable excuses possible.

One sunny spring morning I looked in my calendar and found to my disgust that I had accepted an invitation to a large dinner party in a remote section of Brooklyn. Not only was it going to take me over an hour to get there but also the weather was enticing me to spend the day in the park—after which I knew I would be ready for a quiet evening at home. I thought for a few minutes about the most gracious way to cancel. I could always say I was getting a cold, but I had used that excuse too much during the recent flu season. Finally, inspired by an odd dream I had had the night before, I decided on something unusual. I dialed my friend Andrea.

"Hi. I know you are going to think I am totally wacko, but I had this very strong dream last night—it had a kind of vision quality about it. I dreamt that I was on my way to a dinner somewhere and the car drove off a bridge and I drowned. I woke up so scared I couldn't go back to sleep. I'm sorry, I know it sounds ridiculous, but I don't feel like going anywhere tonight. I'm just too spooked to go out."

This wasn't, strictly speaking, true. And of course this excuse made me sound a little flaky. But so what? Sometimes you have to be willing to sacrifice your own image in order to protect the other person's feelings. Other New Age excuses: "A psychic told me if I went out tonight something bad would happen."

"My horoscope is horrendous for tonight. I have to stay in."
Or, to get out of doing a favor: "My energy is off today. I really
want to do this for you when I am feeling clearer." The very
weirdness of this ruse makes people accept it—even as they are
inwardly shaking their heads, wondering what crazy thing you'll
be into next.

(**Warning:** I guess I don't have to tell you that unless your
employer is an enlightened soul, you should probably not try
this with him or her. Also, don't overuse this excuse. When it
comes to the spiritual arena, it may not be good for your karma
to cry wolf too many times.)

AN ENCYCLOPEDIA OF EXCUSES

Many of the excuses below are variations of—or distant relatives to—the classics. There are basically only nine or ten excuses in the world—the rest is all window dressing. However,
that window dressing is as important to your dodge as sauce is
to pasta.

Always remember rule number one about lying—try to stay
close to the truth when fabricating. If you don't—either because
you can't think of anything close to the truth or because you
think it will be fun to tell a more daring lie—then you'd better
have a darn good memory.

- ALARM CLOCK CALAMITIES:
  "The alarm never went off!"
  "I set it to P.M. instead of A.M."

"My electricity went off in the middle of the night and screwed up my alarm clock."

• BLISSFULNESS:

"I am so in love that I don't even know where I am or what I'm doing!"

"I was meditating . . . [big smile here] . . . am I late?"

"I'm celebrating today! I'll have to get back to you with that tomorrow—today [is my birthday/is my anniversary/I got a raise/we closed on the house/passed the bar/my divorce is final]."

• THE CODGER DODGE:

"Oh, *please*. I'm too old for that!"

• THE DOGGIE DODGE:

"I would love to come but my dog is sick [has to go to the vet/never leaves my side/just bit a neighbor]."

• THE EYE EXCUSE:

"I would love to look at your [baby pictures/poetry/love letter to your boss] but unfortunately I broke my glasses [don't have my reading glasses/don't have my contacts in/have drops in my eyes]."

• FAMILY EMERGENCIES:

"My daughter is in trouble at school; I have to go talk to the principal right away!"

"I have to take my [family member] to the doctor." (The eye doctor or the dentist are both good for this excuse as they both could result in the incapacity of the patient without being too serious.)

• GIFT GIVING:

"No, I don't believe I *have* finished that assignment—but I have a present for you!"

"I am sorry, I will not be able to come to the bridge party, after all but please accept this gift as an apology."

• HOME REPAIRS:

"We would love to have you stay with us but the place is under renovation[being painted/the plumbing is being fixed]. The contractor says he's starting next week so we have to be prepared but . . . who knows?"

• INSOLVENCY:

"We were planning on coming out for the wedding but we are in bad financial straits right now."

"I'm sorry I can't deal with anything right now. I just found out I bounced my rent check."

• JURY DUTY:

"Sorry, I've got jury duty that week."

"My assistant has been on jury duty and everything is a total mess without him here. . . ."

• KISSING:

"Someone new kissed me today and I am in a fog."

"We'll have to talk about that sometime, but right now—kiss me!"

- **Laundry Lies:**

"I know I am overdressed but [the laundry machine broke/ all my regular clothes are at the laundry]."

"Sorry I'm so late—the waitress at lunch spilled tomato soup on my shirt so I had to go buy another one for our four o'clock meeting."

- **The Massage Dodge:**

"I would love to come but I hurt my back and I had to schedule an emergency session with my chiropractor."

"Sorry; I had a really intense massage today and it's made me a little spacey."

- **Nihilism:**

"Sorry, it's not you—it's just that I don't see the point of anything anymore."

"I have decided I hate people. I am never leaving my house again. Don't take it personally."

- **The Oven Escape:**

"I am almost positive I left the oven on."

- **The Pharmaceuticals Ploy:**

"I am not going to be able to give that presentation; I accidentally took too many allergy pills [painkillers, muscle relaxants, cold tablets, etc.] and now I'm feeling woozy."

- **Quality Time:**

"I have to spend some quality time with [insert name of anyone you know here] or our relationship is going to fall apart."

- **ROMANCE RUSES:**

"Sorry, we're having a romantic weekend just for two."

"I know you'll understand that I have to cancel, but I've just been asked out by a very rich single man."

"You don't understand! My lover is in from Sweden!"

- **STINGS AND BURNS:**

"A wasp stung me and my whole leg swelled up; I can barely walk."

"Both of us fell asleep on the beach and we got the worst sunburn—we can't even put clothes on."

"I was all set to have you over to dinner tonight but I burned my hand on some hot grease this morning and I'm afraid I'm in too much pain to cook. Can we reschedule?"

- **THE TRAVEL DODGE:**

"I'm afraid I have to cancel. I have to go out of town on business."

"I have to cut the evening short. I'm on the early shuttle."

"I would *love* to come to your daughter's drum recital but I think that's the weekend I'm out of town."

- **UFO SIGHTINGS:**

"You may not believe this but I saw this huge group of people by the side of the road all looking up at the sky. ... ."

"I was abducted by aliens. They say hi."

- **VISITING A SICK FRIEND:**

"I had to take a friend to the emergency room."

"I had to go donate some blood."

"Sorry, I have to leave early in order to get to the hospital before visiting hours end."

• THE WEATHER:
"The house was hit by lightning and the phone went out."
"All the roads were flooded out . . . we had to stay an extra night."
"The driveway was a sheet of ice [mountain of snow/swimming pool]."
"The pollen count today has really got me feeling off."

• X-RATED EXCUSES:
"The most amazing thing happened to me. I met this woman and we went home and made love all night long. It was a once in a lifetime thing. So I know you can appreciate why I am late [unprepared/forgot about the meeting/not dressed/disheveled/bleary-eyed/calling to cancel]."

"It's been so great having you guys stay with us, but the thing is I'm ovulating now and, well, my husband and I have to have the run of the house, if you know what I mean. Can we help you find a hotel?"

• YARD WORK:
"I have to trim the hedges [mulch the flower bed/work in the garden/cut the grass/cut down a tree/rake the leaves/shovel snow]."

• ZOOLOGY:
"I was just walking out the door when my daughter and I discovered a wounded bird on the front path; so naturally

we had to bring it in and get it settled before we left."

"Hey, there's a bear [wild dog/wolf/rabid bat] outside my front door and I'm not going *anywhere!*"

THE DOUBLE DODGE AND THE
HODGEPODGE DODGE

Sometimes even the best excuses won't hold water. You might tell someone you are jet-lagged, forgetting that they happen to know you only flew from Boston to New York. You might tell a guy you can't date him because you have a big hairy boyfriend, only to have the guy say, "Who cares!" In order to cover all his bases, an artful dodger will sometimes construct a dodge out of more than one excuse.

The Double Dodge works this way: Let's say you borrow a friend's car for the weekend and someone smashes into you in a parking lot, bending the front fender. Because the friend from whom you borrowed the car is fairly persnickety about said car, you decide to take it into the shop and have it fixed before returning it so she won't find out (and you won't have to hear about it for the rest of your life). When she calls to ask you when you are going to bring the car back, you are forced to stall, since the auto repair shop isn't going have it ready until tomorrow. "I was planning on bringing it over this evening," you say as convincingly as you can, "but Martha here has just informed me we are supposed to be at a dinner party about ten minutes ago, so now I won't have time. I'll swing by with it tomorrow."

"Actually," the friend responds, much to your dismay, "I am

going to be in your neighborhood with my sister tonight so I'll just have her drive me by and pick it up. I'll use my spare keys." Uh-oh. Dodge number one has failed. You would be toast at this point if you didn't have a spare excuse in your dodger's trunk.

"Okay, you got me," you say, laughing casually. "The truth is I need the car for one more night. I thought since I had it, I'd pick up the Smiths on the way to the dinner and we'd all go in style for once. I was afraid to come right out and ask you after you were nice enough to let me have the car for the whole weekend. And now the Smiths are counting on us to pick them up."

A powerful one-two punch, the Double Dodge is most effective if you use the less noble excuse as your failsafe. That way the dodgee thinks he has at last uncovered the truth. In other words, if you decide to take the day off just to relax and you say you have the flu, when you are caught healthily jogging in the park, you then say you actually had a doctor's appointment that morning but you didn't want anyone to know. Or when you tell a bore at a cocktail party you have to get a drink, and the bore points out that your glass is still full, you smile as if confessing and say that actually someone has just arrived whom your boss instructed you to talk to—that the drink excuse was just your way of being polite.

Unlike the Double Dodge, the Hodgepodge Dodge unleashes several excuses at once—all in one powerful torrent. It's similar in its energy level to the Terrible Horrible Very Bad Day (see page 60) but its power is in the quantity and coincidence of your excuses rather than in their being misfortunes. The Hodgepodge Dodging of a long-standing social engagement might go something like this:

"Sheila! I meant to call you. I met the man of my dreams yesterday—at least I think he might be—and I totally forgot to call you about the dinner tonight! Which I couldn't have anyway because the storm blew my phone out yesterday; they've just finally got it working again. In any case now I'm getting the flu so I really shouldn't come and infect everyone. Which actually works out just as well because I have an unexpected out-of-town guest coming to stay with me—he's on his way at this very moment. I'll call you when things calm down!" (A less frenetic Hodgepodge: "Listen: I'm not feeling well, I have a lot of work to do, my wife isn't speaking to me, and frankly I want to watch the play-offs anyway.")

No matter what excuse you use, it's not a bad idea to try to make it a self-fulfilling prophecy (except, of course, for the sick excuse). That way you never get found out and you never feel guilty. I know someone who always discovers a household project that desperately needs to be done—one that can be completed only when the kids are out of the house—in order to avoid going to his in-laws. Then he actually does the project while the family is away. This makes it virtually impossible for him to ever get caught in his dodge. Of course, after fifteen years of home repairs, his in-laws might be getting just a *little* suspicious.

CHAPTER 6

✺

The Quick Draw:
Emergency Tactics

Here's another nice mess you've gotten me into.
—STAN LAUREL IN
THE LAUREL-HARDY MURDER CASE

Having good excuses is one thing; being able to come up with one on the spur of the moment is another. If there is one thing predictable about life, it's that it is unpredictable. There are pitfalls where you least expect them. You may not even see the need for dodging until someone is standing in front of you, demanding something you had no idea he or she was going to expect of you. When you are caught completely off guard it can be hard to think of a feasible excuse. The artful dodger needs something specially designed for emergencies, when there is no time to prepare—and no time to lose.

SMOKE AND MIRRORS:
FLATTERY AND OTHER DIVERSIONS

When most of us are suddenly confronted with something troublesome, our first instinct is to flap our hands at it, conversationally speaking, to make it go away. In fact, we *can* often move the other person swiftly away from the danger area by following this instinct and creating some kind of diversion. Although it requires quick reflexes, diverting people usually takes less brain power—not to mention less dishonesty—than previously discussed dodging techniques. Many of us have used this dodge since we were children. However, as "I think I hear my mother calling!" is effective only if you are seven years old and in your own backyard, here are some harmless and easy methods for distracting, de-intensifying, or derailing people.

Flattery

There is nothing like flattery to smooth over any situation. It's the oldest diversionary trick in the book; social butterflies have been breezing through life with it for centuries. It is also a particularly good emergency weapon. If, for example, someone is about to "go postal" on you, gushing over her new hairdo ("Wow! You've got to give me the name of your stylist—you look like a billion dollars!") could very well turn her rampage into a passing comment. Flattery works on the theory that no one ever gets enough of it. It's like throwing bloody meat to hungry Dobermans. Or, put in a slightly more genteel way, it's like projecting love instead of fear.

Naturally, all compliments have to be tailored to the individual who is receiving them, but here are some examples:

FOR QUESTIONS YOU DON'T WANT TO ANSWER

"I can't think straight when in the presence of such physical perfection."

"Sorry . . . your eyes are so distracting . . . I've lost my train of thought."

"What an excellent question. Leave *you* to think of that. Now we know why they hired you."

FOR EVADING EVENTS

"I can't *believe* I have to cancel! I love your parties. They are the high point of my social life. I'm so disappointed!"

"I was so sorry not to see you get your award. But I have to tell you, buddy, I am really proud of you. Actually I'm proud to *know* you!"

FOR DODGING RESPONSIBILITY

"You forget I am not as brilliant [experienced/savvy/perceptive] as you are. I may not be able to. . . ."

FOR AVOIDING SUBJECT MATTER, INTRODUCTIONS, ETC.

"Hello handsome! You are looking very Armani-ish tonight! Better watch out, there are a lot of hungry females around . . . oh no—don't even *try* talking about serious matters when you are looking like that!"

"You two should really talk—seeing as how you are both so incredibly talented! Introduce yourselves, I'll be back in a minute."

"Have you lost weight?" (**Note:** For 99 percent of all women, hearing this line will stop them dead in their tracks, put a smile on their faces, and make them forget everything else for at least ten minutes. This is guaranteed.)

The Pole Vaulter

A Pole Vaulter is someone who is a facile topic jumper and a master of the non sequitur. People who can change subjects drastically and in the blink of an eye—without coming off as either demented or terribly rude—command amazing power in all their interactions. If you can switch subjects well, you can actually leap over, rather than having to dodge, the incoming difficulty.

A fairly pedestrian subject change might be something like "My sales quota sheet certainly needs to be discussed. But before I forget, Mr. Brown called me up with the most astounding news about the second quarter. . . ." Or "Well, I don't know about that, but I do know that I'm starving at the moment." More abrupt would be a sudden interjection like "Have you heard that the president is getting a divorce?"—which, even if it isn't true, is intriguing enough to lead someone off the track.

Some changes of subject are more aggressive than others. If someone is about to bring up the touchy topic of your soon-to-be ex-wife in front of your girlfriend, you might interrupt him with an alarming non sequitur like "Excuse me, but is that a mole? On your cheek there? You better get that checked out, that doesn't look too good." (Moral: Love is swell, but in a pinch fear is a great little helper.) Other generic non sequiturs include "You know, I love your voice"; "I'm so dizzy. Is it hot in here?" "You weren't breast-fed, were you?" "Wait—I just this second remembered a strange dream I had last night," or even "I'm having déjà vu."

The Rubber Ball

This is a less than 100 percent effective technique but it appeals to many people—especially those who hate to lie. The Rubber Ball (otherwise known as "the Psychiatrist") is the well-known practice of asking a question instead of answering what you've been asked. For example, if a person in your sculpture class asks you if you are single and you'd rather not tell him, you smile and respond with "Do I look like I'm single?" Often a slight tone of irony (but not sarcasm, please—arrogance won't help your dodge here) will help confuse and deter the questioner. If your boss asks you why you are late coming into work, ask him, "Am I late?" If he contends that you certainly *are* late, that it is in fact 10:30, you say, "Is it really ten-thirty?" Even when he begins to get irritated and asks you, "Yes, and do you see anyone else here waltzing in at ten-thirty?" continue your Rubber Ball dodging and venture an "I don't know . . . is everyone else here already?" If your "bounce" works, by the time he gets through parrying your questions, your boss will have lost the energy to chastise you—or at least have given you time to decide how you are going to answer him.

Better Dodging Through Humor

If you are a funny person you can dodge a lot of issues just by being funny. Humor can help keep you afloat if you are in hot water. It also works well as a secondary tactic. In other words you might dodge something using the Absentminded Professor technique (see Chapter 4), but spruce it up with a humorous line: "I think I'm having a senior moment." Recent scientific tests have shown that negative ions caused by anger, disappointment, anxiety, and incessant invitations are neutralized to some extent by humor (okay, I made this up but it sounds good).

Of course, no one can teach someone else to be funny, but here are some typical humorous responses for getting out of tight spots, stalling for time, or smoothing over an error.

"I *hate* when this happens."

"How about never? Does that work for you?"

"Macho law forbids me from admitting I'm wrong."

"Someday we'll look back on this, laugh nervously, and change the subject."

"Is is time for your medication or mine?"

"That wasn't me—that was my wounded inner child."

"You know how there are some days you should have stayed in bed? I'm having a whole year like that."

MYSTERIOUS MELODRAMA

Okay, I have something to confess. Something that may damage my personal reputation and my social prowess. This trick is my favorite dodge, and I use it all the time.

The Mysterious Melodrama suits me to a tee, as I am really a frustrated actress at heart. It is a dodge that can get you out of harm's way and at the same time infuse your life with an exciting little glow for a moment or two. Best of all, you can create melodramas for almost any situation:

SCENE ONE: You are on the phone with your brother-in-law. When the conversation gets around to his mounting debts, and you feel pretty certain he is about to hit you up for money, you interrupt him tersely: "Hold on . . . someone's just come into my office . . . [muffled voice] Oh my god, gotta go!" Hang up. Don't call back. When your brother-in-law calls you back, you are not available—you are "away from the office on urgent business." When he does finally track you down and asks you what happened, you shake your head, look up at the ceiling and say, "What a *disaster* that was. Unfortunately there's a confidentiality issue involved so I can't disclose details. Not even to you."

SCENE TWO: You have been invited to a party you suddenly don't want to attend but feel guilty canceling, and you can't think of a good excuse. Your host is giving you directions to his house on the phone when suddenly you exclaim, "Uh-oh . . . don't tell me you live in *that* neighborhood. I . . . I'm sorry but . . . I can't be seen in that neighborhood. I can't tell you why . . . I'm really sorry, I had no idea that's where you lived."

SCENE THREE: You are having difficulty focusing in a meeting. You have given two wrong answers and are now stumped at the question your supervisor has just thrown at you. "I'm really sorry," you say, "the truth is that someone (I don't want to tell you who) was just really abusive to me before the meeting and it's thrown me a bit. I haven't fully regained my equilibrium."

SCENE FOUR: You are sitting on a park bench, sobbing your eyes out over a breakup with your boyfriend, even though it's been months since it happened. Suddenly you hear a voice—it's him! Unfortunately for you he is arm in arm with his new girlfriend. "What's wrong?" he asks you. You answer: "I've had some bad news about a family member . . . I can't talk about it . . . in fact, I hate to be rude but I can't really talk right now. . . ."

SCENE FIVE: You are at a community meeting. The issue on the table is whether or not you will be in charge of the community fair this year. It's your turn to do it but you are hoping to get out of it for one more year. One of your neighbors confronts you: "I don't see why you shouldn't do it this year. Everyone else has taken a turn at it." All eyes shift to you. You look down at your lap for thirty seconds, without saying anything. You look grave (even teary-eyed, if you can manage it). Then you say, "For reasons—personal reasons [long pause] that are nobody's business [another long pause] . . . it's very difficult right now . . . it's just [really long pause] not something I can do at the moment."

SCENE SIX: You are at a very tiresome afternoon tea. You've been there only an hour and you wonder how you will ever make it to the petits fours. The answer: You won't. You excuse yourself, use the telephone, then with an air of quiet intensity approach your hostess. "I'm so sorry," you say, throat constricted and lip quivering, "I must . . . take care of something right away." Your goodbye hug conveys a sense of personal crisis.

One of the big advantages of the Mysterious Melodrama technique is that because you haven't given any details, you don't have to remember anything (an important factor if you are someone like me who can't remember what she did yesterday). If the "audience" of your melodrama wants to know later what the heck was happening to you, your confusion and vague answer only add to the performance. ("Oh . . . *man* . . . something really intense was going on. . . . sorry . . . I can't talk about it.")

DODGING THE BAIT AND SWITCH

The bait and switch, as most of us know all too well, is the name of a common sales tactic in which a customer is attracted by the advertisement of a low-priced item but is then encouraged to buy a higher-priced one. It's a very clever trap that has drawn all of us in at one time or other. But it doesn't happen only in retail.

A woman I interviewed, Brenda, told me of a bait and switch perpetrated on her by one of her neighbors. Brenda had just moved into the building and naturally wanted to get off on the right foot with them. When one of them asked her casually a week after she moved in if she would be able to look after a pet rabbit while the family was away for a weekend, she said she wouldn't mind at all.

The weekend of the rabbit-sitting was only two days away when the neighbor invited her over to introduce her to "Bugsy" and get the keys. After showing her where the rabbit food was kept, the neighbor handed her a sheet of paper with phone numbers on it. "The vet's number is there, as well as the nearest animal emergency room," she said. "The thing is that Bugsy hasn't been feeling too well. If she hasn't gone to the bathroom by Saturday night, the vet said, she could die. So it's very important that . . ." Brenda listened to the rest of the details about the care of the sick rabbit in a growing panic. She wasn't prepared for this! She had expected it to be a simple food-and-water favor. She certainly didn't want to be responsible for the life or death of this rabbit.

The best way to disentangle yourself from a sticky bait and switch trap is to use the same tactics on the person who set the trap. Thus Brenda—who thinks very quickly on her feet—interrupted the neighbor in the middle of some instructions on how to search the rabbit cage for pellets and, smiling agreeably, said, "You know, I really should have brought my daughter over here to hear all this, since she is the one who is actually going to be doing the rabbit-sitting. Harry and I thought it would be a good experience for her—she's seven—to have a little responsibility like this. We told her we would let her to do it all by herself, let herself in with the key and everything. She is smart as a whip, don't worry. She'll have a grand time." As Brenda hoped, the neighbor blanched at this development. The next day the neighbor called Brenda to tell her their "regular" rabbit-sitter was available after all.

EJECTOR SEAT:
GREAT ESCAPE LINES

Once in a while, most of will experience an interaction so excruciating that we feel we are drowning and must have oxygen immediately. Whether it's in person at a party or on the phone in your office; whether it's from fear, annoyance, repulsion, or just mind-bending boredom; in these rare but urgent cases you need something to help you to get away, fast. (**Note:** The lines below are designed as interrupters, like the ones in the Duck and Cover (see Chapter 3), however, the Ejector Seat escape is—hopefully—permanent so there is no need to concoct a Cover.)

Escape Lines

"I . . . Oh! Sorry but I forgot I was supposed to phone someone an hour ago [meet someone twenty minutes ago]. Gotta run."

"I feel sick . . . Excuse me."

"Someone over there was motioning for you to come over. Yes, over there. You can't see her now but she looked kind of desperate."

"I must get some of that smoked salmon over there before it's all gone!"

"My better half is signaling me. Duty calls!"

"Argh! My contact lens!"

"I think I just lost a filling."

CONSOLATION PRIZE:
THE SEMI-DODGE

As a self-professed expert in the art of dodging, I hate to admit this, but there are times when I have found I really cannot dodge an obligation—not entirely, anyway. Recently a friend I hadn't seen in years E-mailed me to tell me she was coming to town on business. I remembered having a lot of fun with this woman years ago, so without thinking about it too much I invited her for dinner. As the appointed evening drew near, I had occasion to talk to the woman on the phone (she wanted advice on things to do in New York). After the third or fourth phone conversation, I began to realize that we had absolutely nothing in common anymore; that each of us had grown in different directions. I began to get a claustrophobic feeling about the evening, and furthermore I knew that if I did have her to dinner I would spend all day cooking and cleaning. I ran through all my dodging options, but ultimately decided that, considering the circumstances, I would feel too smarmy canceling out altogether.

The night before the dinner I called her. "Listen Sue," I said apologetically. "My day tomorrow has just gotten insane. It turns out I have to go downtown for an afternoon meeting, and I thought maybe since you are going to be downtown, we could meet down there—for a drink?—instead of at my place. It would be easier."

Now, Amy Vanderbilt might say I was being rude, but in my opinion a Semi-Dodge is not as disappointing as a cancel, and it at least shows the person you want to see her. The Semi-Dodge is quite a common technique, though it takes various shapes. Many people will turn a proposed lunch into a coffee date or choose to accept an invitation to the big cocktail party over the lunch for two. And if you feel you really have to go to that second cousin's fourth baby shower, you can always arrive late and leave early.

FREEZE!
WHAT TO DO WHEN YOU ARE CAUGHT DODGING

Face it: It's going to happen to you every once in a while. In spite of all your precautions and your well-honed excuses, you are going to get caught dodging. You are going to tell a client you are in a meeting all afternoon and then you will run into that very client in the Turkish bath. When you stutter inanely about how the meeting was canceled, you'll be able to tell the client does not believe you. If the Double Dodge (see page 69) doesn't work (or you don't remember to to use it) and you don't want to try to bluff it out any further, there are four things you can do to partially recover.

1. SHARE A SECRET: You can offer a personal confidence— preferably something embarrassing, or at least intimate. Like giving up false information when you are being tortured, telling something embarrassing about yourself throws them off the scent because they believe it is the thing you are hiding, because it *is*

like something you would hide. "Well you caught me," you might say to the aforementioned client, leaning back against the steamy wall of the Turkish bath, "but sometimes in life, you have to just go have a steam. I have to confess to you—I hope you won't tell anyone back at the office—that I sneak away like this about once every two weeks or so. Sometimes I like to get beaten with eucalyptus leaves. My wife doesn't even know about it." In this way, even though your dodge has been revealed, the client does not have to take it personally (in other words, he may not suspect that your evasion of him was primary and your steam bath secondary).

2. RETRACT YOUR DODGE: Pretend you were kidding or otherwise downplay your dodge. "I didn't say the meeting was in the office, did I? [laugh] Anyway, nobody really believes that 'in a meeting' excuse, do they?" (Laugh again.)

3. THE ANECDOTAL ANTIDOTE: Distract your dodged client with another dodging story—one that features you as the stooge. You say, "You know, if you think *my* little fib was bad . . ." Then you proceed to recount your anecdote, about the time someone really put one over on you. (I recommend using one of the stories in the Wild Story section on page 133.) The purpose of this tactic is twofold: (1) it hopefully diverts the client, and (2) it reminds him that getting dodged happens all the time.

4. VERBAL FIREWORKS: Confess but do it with a fancy vocabulary. "I am afraid you caught me tergiversating." Or "This is probably going to foment your already low opinion of me." A lot of people are intimidated when you use big words. Or they will just think you are a weirdo and be glad you dodged them after all.

CHAPTER 7

Long-Term Strategies

If a thing is worth doing it is worth doing late.
—FREDERICK OLIVER

Quick fixes are great when you can use them, but unfortunately many of life's more challenging interpersonal problems demand long-term solutions. After all, really tough or touchy situations usually took some time to develop in the first place, so it's not surprising that they may take some time to rectify. Always remember that your ultimate goal is not only your comfort but also the comfort of the person you are dodging. The more carefully and gently you can extricate yourself, the more artful you are as a dodger. Some predicaments will require unwavering focus and stamina; in order to minimize the amount of hurt, you will have to execute your dodge with the painstaking care of a surgeon performing quadruple bypass surgery.

THE SLOWDOWN

No one likes to talk about it, but everyone is familiar with this traditional tapering-off technique. The Slowdown is a popular method of dealing with unsatisfactory relationships, chronic callers, or overly aggressive acquaintances. It's tantamount to backing out of a room after you've realized you shouldn't be there. Here is an example of how this slow-motion fade out is accomplished.

Mary and Mike are good friends with Mike's coworker Tim and Tim's wife, Tina. Both Mary and Mike have always found Tina less likable than Tim; so when Tim and Tina get divorced, Mary and Mike decide that they would like to maintain their relationship with Tim but not necessarily with Tina. For a while they socialize with both separately, but as time goes on, and Tina's open hostility for Tim persists, Mike and Mary resolve to call it quits with Tina.

Mike and Mary don't want to hurt Tina's feelings by dumping her outright, so they gradually begin to scale back on the time they see her. What used to be a once-a-week get-together becomes once every two weeks, then once a month. When Tina calls they are always very nice but usually very busy. When Tina invites them to dinner—asking them to pick the date—Mike and Mary schedule it as far in the future as possible, claiming they are booked. For several months Mary still spends a lot of time talking to Tina on the phone, but less and less time seeing her in person. To keep their Slowdown from being too noticeable, occasionally Mary or Mike initiate a call to Tina to ask how she is and to say they are thinking of her. On the other hand, Mary will often wait until Tina calls two or three times before returning the call—always with apologies for being swamped with work, family, and other obligations. Mike and Mary's attitude toward Tina remains very warm and loving, but eventually Tina becomes someone the couple sees once or twice a year.

The Slowdown can take months (sometimes years) to complete. Like bringing a deep-sea diver gradually up to the surface, you have to recede in very small increments to make this technique virtually pain-free. Your progress may not be completely steady; at some point during the process the victim may suspect what is happening and confront you. During such times you have to be extremely kind, perhaps seeing her once or twice more than you had planned. Obviously, the amount of time and effort you put into this drawn-out dodge will be in direct proportion to how deeply involved you were with the person to begin with. (If it's a family member you could be "slowing down" for a decade!)

THE DANCE OF DEFERMENT

Much of artful dodging is like a dance, but no maneuver is more like a dance than this tactic. One amazing dodger I know, Peter, confided to me about a protracted dodge he was involved in at work, involving a pesky project that he had been assigned. He was supposed to photocopy and circulate the notes from the weekly sales meeting to about thirty people in the company. It wasn't the most urgent job in the world; in fact, most people in the company never read the notes. Nevertheless, the boss was a stickler about things like minutes. Peter absolutely hated this job, which he felt interfered with more important duties.

One week Peter simply didn't distribute the minutes. At the end of the week nothing happened, so Peter neglected to do it the next week too. Finally, in the middle of that week, Peter got an E-mail from his boss, asking him what had happened to the notes of the sales meeting.

And so it began. Peter E-mailed back and said he had been about to do the job but the copier had been in use. When the boss asked Peter again a few days later, Peter laughed and promised he was going to catch up on it soon, but that now he had several weeks' worth of notes and copying them required a larger time slot than he could usually find in the day. Each week the boss—sometimes teasing, sometimes threatening—would inquire where the notes were. Each week Peter had a new, plausible excuse. Now, luckily for Peter, his performance in other areas was exemplary. When last I spoke to him, he was at eight weeks and counting.

Of course, Peter's particular dance is somewhat unusual—and slightly risky. A more common variety of this technique consists of continually putting off a client or friend who wants to see you more than you want to see him. ("I know we said we were going to have lunch this week but I'm totally crazed. Next week for sure.") If you are well practiced at the Dance you are probably using a lot of phrases like "I'll get back to you," "Maybe I'll see you this weekend," "We'll have to grab a cup of coffee next week," "We'll talk soon, I promise," and even the hackneyed "Let's have lunch sometime." A lot of people see this modus operandi as normal operating procedure—even good sport. It can be like having a contest with yourself to see how long you can defer before you have to give up and do something about whatever it is.

(**Warning:** This long-term delaying tactic can be detrimental to your psychological health. Problems tend to get bigger the longer you put them off. Something that may have initially required only a small, inconsequential dodge may necessitate a major troop movement after it has festered for weeks or months. Please make sure you are being an artful dodger and not a pathological procrastinator!)

THE BROKEN RECORD

Once upon a time there was a nice family who lived on a shady street in suburbia. They were a happy but somewhat sloppy family. Unfortunately, their next-door neighbor was a crotchety old man who loved to complain about things. One of the things that bothered him was the front porch belonging to the nice family, which was forever littered with trash, toys, and old furniture.

About once a week the old man would call the nice family up and yell at them. "Your house is an eyesore! When are you going to clean that mess up? Why should we have to look at all that junk on your front porch?" he would rant. Fortunately, the nice family had found a way to deal with this man. Whoever answered the phone when the man called would hand the phone to the mother of the nice family—as she was the one with the most patience.

"I understand what you are saying, Mr. Fitzwater," she

would say sweetly and calmly. "And we'll get to it as soon as we can." At this sentiment, which he had heard so many times before, the old man's rage would escalate. But no matter what he said, the mother of the nice family would repeat the same thing, in the same tone of voice: "Uh-huh, yes . . . I understand what you are saying and we will get to it as soon as we can." The mother of the nice family never, *ever* lost her temper. The porch never got cleaned up. The old man eventually gave up, and the nice family who lived on the shady street in suburbia lived happily ever after.

People who work in complaint or service departments are usually experts at playing the Broken Record. It's not only an effective dodging method but can also be a great spiritual practice. It's like deep breathing or Tai Chi. You remain firmly but gently in your centered place no matter what happens. Listen attentively but keep restating your position. It's amazing how well this works. The person on the other end of the Broken Record may at first become agitated but will almost always relent after a while. Sometimes he will even end up admiring your state of calm.

(**Note:** This is the technique of choice for penultimate dodges like breaking up with someone, quitting your job, or—by many accounts the trickiest one—leaving your therapist. The key to success in these potentially explosive situations is not to allow yourself to be drawn into an argument or to concede to a request that may delay your escape, such as "Let's talk about that next week," or "What do you think you are really running away from?" Just play your good-bye theme until it's the only sound anyone in the room can hear.)

THE PAVLOVIAN DODGE

In his famous "conditioned response" experiment, Ivan Pavlov trained a hungry dog to salivate at the sound of a bell—a bell that was associated with the sight of food. In a similar way, you, the artful dodger, can condition someone to leave you alone.

One of the greatest dodging challenges I have ever had was Chester. Chester is the son of my mother's oldest and best friend in the world. My mother and this friend decided when Chester and I were about three that it would be perfect for everyone if he and I were to end up together. When we were growing up we were made to play together. We went to kindergarten together when we were five, dancing class together when we were nine, and played duets on the piano when we were eleven. I always thought Chester was kind of a dork, but he never chased me around with dead mice or anything, so I put up with him. When I was twelve, as fate would have it, Chester and his family moved away to California.

About three years ago I got a very excited phone call from my mother. Chester had moved to New York. The two mothers worked fast, and within the week I had a date to be reunited with my childhood playmate. If this had been a movie (or even someone else's life) Chester would have somehow matured into a studly but sensitive eligible bachelor—but no such luck. He was still dorky, but he had acquired another less-than-attractive quality—arrogance. He insulted the waiter, he condescended to me, he made blatantly sexist comments, bragged incessantly about his job, and—worst of all—acted as if we were engaged.

In short, I had a serious problem on my hands. Because I did not want it to get back to Chester's mother (whom I dearly love, and who thankfully never reads my books) that I rejected her pride and joy, and because I didn't want to have to explain to my mother that it was my fault that her lifelong dream was never going to happen, I decided the safest way to proceed was with the Pavlovian Dodge.

I began my campaign on our second date. I made sure I was half an hour late. During dinner I knocked my glass of wine into his braised trout. The next time we got together (to go to the theater) I allowed a loud belch to escape from my lips during a quiet moment in the play (this was hard for me to do, as I was raised in the South, but I was keeping my eyes on the prize). I saw Chester about six or seven times, and each time I made sure I did something distasteful. For one entire evening I refrained from smiling. By our last date I could see that he was just going through the motions—that the fire had gone out of his beady little eyes. But just to make sure the programming took, I "accidentally" spilled very hot coffee into his lap when he made a proprietary grab for me on the sofa.

Believe me, every time Chester hears my name he does not salivate. He winces. In fact, just as Pavlov's dog became conditioned not just to the food but to the sight of the technician who provided the food, Chester probably winces when he sees my mother now, too. Our paths are finally disentangled, and Chester believes it was his decision for us to part ways.

CHRONIC COMPLAINTS

This technique really comes under the heading of excuses but because it is enacted over a prolonged period it is considered a long-term strategy. Like buying detergent in the family-size container, using a chronic complaint can afford you lots of dodges for the price of one.

Let's say you are entering a period during which—for one reason or another—you feel you are going to have to do a lot of dodging. What you do is start telling everyone that your phone has been malfunctioning—perhaps because of a new line you are putting in for your computer. (Everyone is used to problems with the phone company.) For the next two weeks or so, you can dodge almost anyone or anything you want by re-gurgitating this excuse. ("You know my phone service has been messed up.") The classics work well for this dodge. "I think I'm getting sick" you say to people on Tuesday. By Wednesday you say you *are* sick, and for two weeks after that, you can be "re-covering" to whomever you need to dodge. The great thing about this technique is that it leaves your options open. Unlike the Closed Door in Chapter 2, you can come out of hiding anytime you like ("The phone's working today!") or ("Suddenly I don't feel that bad!"). Other popular chronic complaints are the Friend in Crisis and Too Much Work at the Office.

CHAPTER 8

The Dirty Dodge:
Getting Someone Else to Do Your Dodging

Pay no attention to that man behind the curtain.
—THE WIZARD IN *THE WIZARD OF OZ*

I have an old college friend who, whenever he is faced with something that takes more than the slightest bit of effort, will announce with glee, "Okay—I'll put a man on that." (He used to say this even when he was in college.) Not surprisingly, he is now CEO of a well-known company. The most sophisticated dodger knows when to get help from other people. Taking cover behind someone else may seem like the coward's way out, but it often makes for the most convincing—even brilliant—evasions.

I have always depended on the kindness of friends. However, as dodging props, friends are secondary in desirability to spouses, who *rule*. Like people with kids, people with live-in mates have a huge dodging advantage—a built-in excuse as well as a built-in partner in crime. Nevertheless, any family member, roommate, or good friend can serve as your first line of defense, your alibi, or your accomplice.

THE SCAPEGOAT: A colleague lent you his favorite basketball (the one signed by Michael Jordan). Now you can't find it and he wants it back. You don't want him to know it might be lost (you remember seeing the neighborhood kids playing with it) for a very simple reason—because he will kill you.

Enter the scapegoat—in this case, your spouse. (Promising to serve in this capacity is part of the marriage contract.) "Sarah put it somewhere and she can't find it. But don't worry. I'll get after her this weekend." The only blame that can be leveled at *you* is that you married the wrong person.

The scapegoat possibilities are endless: "Sorry, I couldn't do my math homework—my roommate accidentally set my book on fire when she was cooking." "I never got your message—my husband forgot to write it down." "Sorry I'm late—my wife sprained her ankle and I had to take her to the doctor." "I would have loved to come but Joe forced me to stay home to help him with his project." "It turns out Sue made another date for us tonight and neglected to tell me." "My mother says I have to be home by six o'clock P.M."

It's crucial, of course, that you inform the scapegoat of any deed she is supposed to have done, if there is even the remotest possibility of the dodgee and the scapegoat having any contact. The last thing you want to hear as you enter your house is your wife on the phone saying, "*What* lost basketball?"

THE COHABITANT CONSULT: This is that handiest of all staving-off techniques, otherwise known as the I Have to Check With My Wife ploy. Perfect for pop invitations, this dodge was ingrained in most of us as children ("I don't know, go ask your mother"). Unlike its first cousin the Duck and Cover (page 35), the Cohabitant Consult allows for the possibility that you may eventually accept the invitation—or that you will "forget" to check with your wife at all, thereby letting the whole thing dissipate.

GOOD COP/BAD COP: A great ruse for couples, but also quite doable with roommates or siblings, this dodge requires a team effort. Let's say you have guests who won't leave your house; you play the good cop while the person who is helping you is the bad cop. Dinner and coffee are long over. When you can't stand it anymore and you are beginning to fear these people will never leave, the bad cop yawns, stands up, and excuses himself with, "I'm afraid I've got to hit the hay. I'm dead on my feet. Goodnight, Bob and Sue. Don't forget to let in the cat, sweetheart." After the bad cop has disappeared, the good cop apologizes for her partner, while emphasizing how much it *is* past his bedtime. Even a total nincompoop of a guest should get the message at this point and pack it in.

Another way to play Good Cop/Bad Cop is to conjure up a relationship "issue" (or better yet, exaggerate an authentic one):

"My husband has been peeved at me lately for not being around [not paying enough attention to him/not letting him use the phone/not putting in enough time with the kids, etc.]." Good Cop/Bad Cop also works like a charm for quick exits: "*I* would love to stay but Charlie is dead on his feet." "I have to hang up— my precocious child is hitting me on the shin with a Teletubby."

USING ASSISTANTS AND COLLEAGUES

Often the main function of your assistant is to serve as a shield between you and the rest of the world. But even if you don't have a trusty girl or guy Friday to bar people from your door, you can usually find a buddy in the office to help you out.

RUNNING INTERFERENCE: When your assistant runs interference for you, you are on the other line, you are in a meeting, you are out to lunch, you are in the executive washroom—anywhere but where the vultures can find you. A good assistant uses some embellishments to effect a convincing dodge. For instance, when asked if you are in, he may say, "Hold on, let me take a look," which is sometimes preferable to "Hold on, I'll see." Ideally, you want the person who is calling for you to get the picture in his mind's eye of the assistant actually going to look for you in your office (under the desk, behind the filing cabinet, out on the ledge). This tends to make the dodged person less suspicious when the assistant inevitably returns and says, "No, he seems to have stepped out." Of course, an artful dodger is never unavailable *all* the time; occasional availability makes the times he does dodge more believable.

RESCUE MISSION: The rescue mission is similar to running interference but here the technique is employed after you are already stuck. Perhaps your office manager has come into your office, planted himself in a chair, and is showing no signs of leaving—or of shutting up. If you are lucky, your assistant will notice what is happening and save you by buzzing you with an "important call." Or a helpful coworker (who hopes you will return the favor sometime) will barge into your office with some "urgent business." I actually know a top executive who has a secret button out of sight under his desk that he can use to signal for help in such a predicament.

THE STAGED DODGE: Because it takes a bit of rehearsing, this maneuver is designed for more difficult problems. To perform this dodge you need to have a prearrangement with the other half of your dodging duo. Then, seemingly by coincidence, your helper calls you or comes in while your dodge target is with you. The point is to let the target overhear what you want him to overhear—that you are called away on urgent business, or that some long-standing commitment you have with the target is now fouled up: "You need me tomorrow? Can't I do it some other time? Gee, I was going to do something with my friend Joe here . . . but if you need me so much . . ."

My favorite case of the Staged Dodge came from someone I interviewed named Jack. Jack would habitually meet blind dates at an upscale establishment where he knew the maître d'. One of the first things he would say to his date would be that he was lucky to have gotten away from work. He would explain that there was a terrible crisis brewing at the office, but that he had managed to slip out without anyone noticing. About ten minutes into the date, Bill, the maître d', would approach their table. "Is everything all right, sir?" he would inquire.

If Jack wanted to escape the date, he would answer, "Yes, Frederick, everything is fine." The maître d' was well rehearsed. By deliberately addressing Bill by the wrong name, Jack had secretly informed the maître d' that he wanted out *A.S.A.P.* A few minutes later Bill would return, acting very apologetic.

"I'm so sorry to intrude, sir, but your office is calling." Feigning annoyance, Jack would tell his date that the office, aware that this club was one of his favorite hangouts, must have tracked him down. Then he would make his apologies and leave.

THE "TASMANIAN DODGE":
SOLICITING STRANGERS

The "Tasmanian Dodge" is a scam used to cast fraudulent ballots in an election. An unmarked ballot is stolen by one voter and delivered to a person outside the polling place who is buying votes. That person marks the ballot and gives it to another voter who in turn deposits it in the ballot box and steals a new ballot to continue the process. While you are not expected to mastermind anything this complicated (or illegal), finding a stranger to help you every once in a while is sometimes warranted and can be extremely effective. Strangers are perfect dupes—no one ever suspects you have enlisted them to help you out of a tough spot.

A relative of mine, I'll call her Leigh, told me that when she was sixteen she was coerced into attending a country club family dance with a thirteen-year-old neighborhood boy. It didn't help a bit that Leigh was five feet six inches at the time and her date was about four feet three inches. She was mortified—as only a sixteen-year-old can be—to be seen dancing with this boy or (worse) to have anyone think he was her boyfriend.

There she was, out on the dance floor, feeling like a piece of luggage being dragged around by an unruly puppy, when suddenly she spotted the proverbial tall, handsome stranger enter the room. Catching the stranger's eye, Leigh—with inspiration born of desperation—mouthed the word "HELP" over her date's shoulder at him. To her delight and utter relief, the newcomer came right over and cut in! (P.S. They went out for about two months, which for many sixteen-year-olds constitutes a long-term relationship.)

I find you can usually recruit strangers at parties to save you from stranger strangers ("Would you please talk to me for a few minutes? That man is bothering me"); or nice passersby on the street to help you dodge other, less nice passersby. Sometimes you don't even have to recruit the strangers; they volunteer. Once I was standing on a street corner waiting for a friend when a bedraggled-looking, inebriated man came weaving up to me.

"Hey . . . wanna . . . come . . . w'me?"

"No thank you." I replied firmly. I turned away, hoping he would get the message. He became more insistent.

"HEY! . . . Gimmee a dollar, y'beautiful . . . wmshshsss . . ."

It was becoming clear to me I wasn't going to get him to go away. I tried saying sharply, "NO!" but he just kept coming closer and getting louder. I looked vaguely around for an escape, wondering if I was going to have to give up waiting for my friend to avoid this person.

Suddenly another man, who was walking along the sidewalk about ten yards away, waved gaily at me and ran up beside us. The newcomer was nice-looking, well dressed, and had a big, welcoming smile on his face.

"Hi!" he said, shaking my hand vigorously, "I am so sorry I'm late! Have you been waiting long?" I felt a little dizzy; I had no idea who this man was. Was I going crazy? Then I noticed he had placed his body in between the bum's and mine. He leaned in close and whispered in my ear, "I saw this guy bothering you . . . you looked as if you needed rescuing."

"Oh! . . . Yes, well, it's about time you got here!" I teased back, playing along. The drunken man mumbled something and moved off down the street, and I thanked the good Samaritan profusely for the dodge-assist.

ENLISTING IMAGINARY PERSONNEL

If you can't find anyone to help you, have no fear. There's no law that says your dodging ally has to be real. Sometimes a fictional person can work just as well—or better. Unlike real people, imaginary people can be at your beck and call, twenty-four hours a day.

SURPRISE VISIT: There is nothing like a surprise visit for cutting short a phone call. (You'd think it would be easy to end a phone call whenever you want, but we all have someone in our lives who seems to be able to talk without ever taking a breath.) The surprise visit can be from an imaginary neighbor or an imaginary friend. You can even prepare a long-winded caller for the interruption a few minutes in advance, by saying, "I just want to let you know I am expecting my friend Debbie any minute so I may have to get off the phone." If you want to carry it off really well you can actually greet the empty air. ("Hi Deb—one second, I'm just getting off the phone.") One man I know, who lives in a rural area where relationships with the UPS man, the postman, and the FedEx woman are very important, uses this dodge all the time. Whenever this man is bored with a phone conversation he will suddenly announce that the UPS or FedEx person is driving up to the house. (The caller is made to understand that a personal visit with this delivery person is expected.)

CREATING COMPETITION: One day not too long ago when I was on the subway trying to explain to a persistent man why I didn't date people who tried to pick me up on the subway, I realized that the easiest course of action for dodging amorous advances is not the truth. It is so much kinder and quicker to invent a husband—or at least a burly boyfriend. After all, who benefits from a complicated rebuff? If you've gone out with someone a few times and you want to bail, why not tell the person you are going back to your fiancé (who in reality does not exist), and that if it weren't for this unexpected reuniting, *of course* you would have loved to go out with him or her again? (The classic "it's not you, it's me" kiss-off is often the gentlest way to reject someone, as long as you make it believable.) You can Create Competition for dodging a job opportunity ("I'd love to work in your raw sewage process plant but I have another offer"), or for ducking a drop-in visitor ("Ordinarily I'd love to see you but I've got someone over here right now").

MULTIPLE PERSONALITY: I personally know at least four people who have pretended to be their own secretaries when they didn't have an assistant handy to be their watchdog/barrier. Believe it or not, people do this by disguising their voice in some way (usually their voices become louder and brasher—following some Hollywood stereotype for secretaries). Now, if *I* know four people who use this dodge, there must be a lot of people in the world who are doing it—though I imagine you'd have trouble getting people to admit it. It can be embarrassing to get caught pretending to be someone else, especially if the person who catches you is the chairman of the board. In your own home, it's a different story: I have a friend who regularly deals with telephone solicitors by pretending to be the house boy, the gardener—or any other servant that pleases his fancy that day.

UNDER ORDERS: This technique is useful for dodging undesirable conversations. Like a sequestered juror, your dodging line is a clear and definite "I'm not allowed to talk about it." Whether it's your doctor, your lawyer, your agent, your business manager, your boss, your accountant, your real estate dealer, your stockbroker, your spouse, or your therapist, it's someone who in this specific situation is an authority figure. Being "under orders" allows you to say no to the subject without saying no; it's someone *else* in charge who is really saying no. If you get good at this you can do it without even revealing who has sworn you to secrecy: "I'm not supposed to talk about that. I can't tell you why."

NOT MY DECISION: Some salespeople can be aggressive to the point of unpleasantness. When you come to that awkward moment when you feel a salesperson is trying to force you into buying something, remember that even if you live alone you can say, "I'll have to come back with my husband [mother/son/daughter]." It's very freeing once you understand that invoking fantasy people in your life doesn't hurt anyone—and can help you a lot. To telephone solicitors, for example, try "My wife always makes all those decision," and hang up. (I know someone who goes further: "My psychotherapist handles these kinds of calls. Call back later.")

Of course you can always tell the truth, and explain to the salesman that you a) aren't ready to buy, b) want to look at what the competition has, and c) want to think about it; but salespeople are trained to argue those points away. It saves a lot of time and energy to invent a partner with whom you can share life's important decisions. Just don't start setting a place for him at dinner.

CHAPTER 9

∾

Telecommunication Tricks

*Technology—the knack of so arranging the world
that we don't have to experience it.*
—MAX FRISCH

Sometimes I long for the days before answering systems, fax
machines, and E-mail; when—protected and private in your
own home—you could just let the phone ring without answering, and scrawl "return to sender" across the backs of unwanted
letters. The more technology we have the more dodging we
have to do. The more dodging we have to do, the more technology we need to help us dodge. It's a vicious circle. In this
modern age everyone is expected to be "reachable" by some
electronic method or other. It's assumed that you are regularly
checking your phone messages, downloading your E-mail, and
changing the batteries in your beeper and cell phone. This
makes life much more complicated—and increases the need for
artful dodging.

ANSWERING MACHINES AND VOICE MAIL: THE ULTIMATE PROTECTION

Undoubtedly, answering machines and voice mail are the best technical support system a dodger can have. Many people would never think of picking up the phone without letting their machine screen the call first. While actual machines give you the advantage of being able to hear a person leaving a message live, the telephone company's voice answering system allows someone to leave you a message while you are on the phone with someone else. The phone company feature that is actually detrimental to your dodging health is Call Waiting, which affords someone whom you may wish to avoid an excellent chance of getting through to you while you are on the phone with someone else—if only for a minute. (For those people who like to use their Call Waiting feature as a hang-up technique, *you don't actually need Call Waiting to do this*. See page 112.)

A friend of a friend of mine, a lawyer, has an excellent phone setup. He has two phone lines, with two different numbers. Each of the numbers is listed under a different version of his name; the law firm has only one of these numbers—the one to which an answering machine is attached. He never answers this phone on the weekends—ever.

The usefulness of automatic answering systems is obvious; you can talk to people when you are ready to talk to them and not before. You can find the information the caller needs before you call her back. And best of all, if you are smart you can avoid talking to the person at all by returning his call when you know he is not in. Many executives race to their offices at 7:30 A.M. in order to return all their messages from the day before and still not talk to a soul. (Although lunchtime is also an excellent time to not reach people.) Unfortunately, they may find another eager beaver doing the same thing—much to both parties' chagrin.

I know of only one person who does not have an answering machine or voice mail of any kind. It irritates everyone in her life, but she is old-fashioned and feels the phone is there for her to reach other people, not for people to reach her. She rarely picks up her phone when she is at home. At a result, hardly anyone calls her at home anymore. I suspect she has, in fact, used this Luddite practice of hers as a passive-aggressive dodging technique—to great effect, I might add.

THE CALL WAITING DODGE AND
OTHER HANG UP TECHNIQUES

Sometimes the phone can seem like your lifeline; other times it can be as invasive as having an unwanted foot stuck in your door. If you don't want to be constantly hiding behind your voice mail, there are going to be times when you pick up the phone and know immediately that it was a mistake of gargantuan proportions. And if it *is* your ex-husband calling to relate the gory details of his latest affair, you may need a way to hang up on him without actually slamming down the phone.

The Call Waiting Dodge

One of a dodger's best tricks is the Call Waiting Dodge. This works whether you have Call Waiting or not (unless the caller happens to know for a fact you don't have Call Waiting).

INSTRUCTIONS

Step one: Create the illusion of a Call Waiting signal by lightly tapping the receiver button. Be careful not to disconnect the person, which can happen if you press down too hard or too long. If you are one of the few people in America who still have a dial phone, you can rotate the dial slightly to imitate the Call Waiting signal. (Note: If you live in one of the areas that now have a silent Call Waiting signal, you can omit this step entirely.)

Step two: As if embarrassed or annoyed, interrupt your caller with "Oh . . . I'm sorry, can you hold on? It's my Call Waiting."

Step three: If your phone doesn't have a "hold" button (many phones do), place your hand securely over the mouthpiece for approximately fifteen seconds.

Step four: Carefully take your hand off the mouthpiece. Say, "Hi. Listen, I've got to take this. It's long distance [it's my sick grandmother/it's my boss/my long-lost daughter]."

Step five: Hang up quickly. *Don't* promise to call back. Your object is a total dodge, not just a Duck and Cover.

(**Note:** If, during the procedure, you accidentally disconnect your caller, wait until he calls back and then say, "I am sorry, I think there's something wrong with my phone, I . . ." and hang up again. Keep doing this until he gives up entirely, filled with pity for you and your faulty phone system.)

The Hang Up Voice

The Hang Up Voice is a bit like hypnotizing the person on the other end of the line. Your voice must seduce or lull him into getting off the phone. Your attitude must not just convey but must positively *drip* with good-bye energy. Practice these conversation-ending phrases, using the effective sliding down cadence:

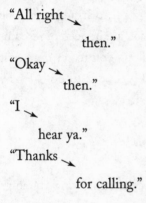

"All right ↘

then."

"Okay ↘

then."

"I ↘

hear ya."

"Thanks ↘

for calling."

The Phony Page

A man I'll call Ted has developed a brilliant escape system. He and his assistant share an office. The office, which is in a bottling plant, is equipped with a company-wide paging/intercom system, so that supervisors who might be checking on the machinery can be easily located. Whenever Ted is on a call with—to use his term—a "chatterbox," he silently signals to his assistant across the room. The assistant sounds the pager buzzer (which the caller can plainly hear) and then gets on the intercom and announces, "Ted Tompkins—you have an urgent call from . . ." (which the caller can also plainly hear). This allows

Ted to hang up almost immediately, without any trouble at all. He doesn't have to worry about bringing the conversation to a logical conclusion or dealing with an issue that was being discussed. Ted confessed to me with a sly smile that on a couple of occasions when his assistant was out of the room, he has gotten up from his desk while the caller was still talking away and paged *himself* on the intercom!

Less spectacular but just as sneaky are the fake beeper and cell phone interruptions. It is fairly simple to arrange for someone to either beep or call you when you are in need of rescuing. Some pagers have a function that allows you to set the beeper to go off at a certain time. Then all you need to do is look at it, act annoyed, and make a quick exit.

The Accident

If you are into high drama and the caller is making you angry anyway, try making crashing sounds into the phone (nonbreakable things like pots and pans work well for sound effects), then hang up. When the person calls back tell him you dropped the phone on your foot and you can't talk because it hurts too much. (**Warning:** This is for dire emergencies only, as it's entirely possible that the person will show up at your front door with an ice pack.)

Fun with Telemarketers

Everyone hates telemarketers. Hating them is one of the things that binds us together as a society. I have already mentioned various ways to dodge telemarketers, but here are a few other tips.

First of all, if you are an upright, no-nonsense type of person, you may just want to go the straight route and tell whomever that you don't accept sales calls of any kind on the phone and you are officially requesting that they take you off their list. It is the law (in most places anyway) that they must comply with this request.

I, however, sometimes do not have either the patience or the inclination to do this. So here are a few other fun things to try before hanging up:

- You can almost always tell it's a sales call when you hear that long pause after you say hello. (This is because the telemarketer computer dials several numbers at a time.) If you hear this telltale pause, hang up before they can even get to you.
- Pretend to be a three-year-old: "Ya wanna play wi' me, mister?"
- Tell them you are glad they called because you have something you want to sell them. Give them an aggressive sales pitch until they hang up.
- Start singing at the top of your lungs. ("I'm Just a Girl Who Can't Say No" and "I Feel Pretty" are my personal favorites.)
- Give them sympathy. Cut them off in the middle of their pitch and say, "You must hate your job. How do you do it? Is your boss right there, watching you? Do you get in trouble if you don't follow the script?"

DODGING ON-LINE

The Internet has created a whole new kind of communication—
a middle area somewhere between writing and talking. Like all
other kinds of communication, E-mail is both a good tool for
dodging and a thing we sometimes need to dodge. The world of
E-mail is relatively new and constantly changing—the Wild
West of our time. This flux means more dodging leeway. Use it!

DELAY: One of the best things about E-mail as a dodging device
is the delay factor. Receiving something via E-mail—especially
personal or home E-mail—can be a perfect shield, because no
one can ever be sure of your E-mail habits. Some people check
their E-mail five times a day, some five times a month. When
someone wants to know why you haven't gotten back to her, you
can always lie and say you haven't checked your E-mail in a while.
In some cases a delay of as long as several weeks can even be
excused; people on long vacations could conceivably be away from
their E-mail for that long. (**Note:** The sender of an AOL E-mail
can tell exactly when another AOL user has read his E-mail. So
if you are dodging someone in particular, don't open that person's
E-mail message until you are ready to deal with it. I know someone who switched to a different I.S.P. solely because he didn't
like being exposed in this fashion. The "Return Receipt" function
on many providers does the same thing, often without the recip-
ient's knowing about it, so beware.)

DODGING CONFRONTATION: E-mail is also a good way to dodge
direct confrontation or to ease tense situations. A divorced couple told
me they negotiated their divorce entirely by E-mail. They said it dif-

116

fused the negativity, it was not as formal and therefore not as scary as letter writing, but it still allowed both parties time to think so that neither one got overemotional. A lot of people also use E-mail for rejecting people romantically. There's no sweating, no clearing of the throat, and no wondering what to wear to the confrontation. (And in cyberspace, no one has to see you cry.)

LOST IN CYBERSPACE? A would-be dodger will try to get away with anything. Many people used to claim on a fairly regular basis that they didn't receive messages. Now, perhaps at the beginning of this whole E-mail craze it was possible that you or your server was confused enough to lose E-mail. But not anymore. In fact, we hardly ever hear the Lost in Cyberspace excuse anymore. On the other hand, people do change their E-mail addresses more often than they change any other address or number, so anonymity is still possible if you need to go into hiding.

ABOUT NOT ANSWERING: Is it acceptable to simply not return E-mail? The rules for E-mail are not the same as for phone calls. Certainly you don't have to bother answering those incessant group E-mails (junk mail from friends). Unless there is a question asked of you, you are under no obligation to respond. If someone "Instant Messages" you while you are on-line, a simple "I'm too busy to talk," suffices. People should assume you have some other purpose to be on-line than to hang around and wait for people to I.M. you. Instant Messaging is one of the most intrusive things ever invented. (People may as well be sticking their head into your living room windows.) I did learn a good trick from someone recently, if you want to ward off an unwanted Instant Messenger. You simply do not respond; then, later when the person sees you in person and asks you why you wouldn't answer him on-line, you say that lots of times (most of the time) you are either away from your computer or you are letting someone else use your Internet access.

HOW TO BLAME TECHNOLOGY
AND GET AWAY WITH IT

Technology is really the artful dodger's best friend—not because it works but because it so often doesn't. Goodness knows what people are going do when the communications industry finally gets the bugs out of cell phones. Gone will be one of the world's easiest dodges: the "You're breaking up" escape. It's astounding to me that this ruse works at all, considering how many cell phone users seem to employ it. But that's the great thing about blaming technology—you never know for sure. Half the time you really *are* breaking up. (Almost every day I see some person shaking, hitting, or cursing at her cell phone.)

I must say a word here about faking the disconnect, which can be done on either a cell phone or a regular phone. You have to make certain you push the "drop" button (or the receiver button) when *you* are in the middle of a sentence—not when the other person is speaking. This tactic, called (for some unknown reason) the Young Lawyer's Trick, works because people can never quite believe you would cut *yourself* off. When they call back, do not answer (if possible). This completes the illusion that you are "out of order."

Another fine way to blame technology is to claim personal incompatibility with your system (in other words, to say you are a bumbling idiot). While hot-shot technophiles may not be able to handle the pride wounding involved with admitting they are having trouble operating their machines, I have often heard the excuse "I couldn't call you back because I accidentally erased all my messages," and believed it. Similar dodges include: "I accidentally deleted my E-mail addresses," and "Believe it or not, I wrote the whole report last night and then forgot to hit the 'save' button!"

For anyone working out of her home, another good techno-malfunction ruse is to call whomever you want to dodge and tell him you are having electricity and/or phone difficulties. This ensures that he won't call you—rendering your home office a safe haven. A friend of mine goes so far as to call her victims from a pay phone (complete with heavy street noise), just to make her technical difficulty sound authentic. Of course, you can also turn the dodge around and try to convince other people its *their* technology that has failed. "I tried calling you several times and got no answer. Your machine must be broken" is a common, if somewhat weak, ploy and is often followed by the even weaker, "Of course, maybe I dialed wrong." This tactic is not recommended unless you have reason to think the person has recently had problems with her answering system.

Without question, the most convincing, useful, all-encompassing, empathy-inspiring dodge in today's microchip universe is the invoking of computer problems. People never blink an eye but instead swallow it hook, line, and sinker when you tell them that your computer is messed up in some way. Whether the screen is frozen, the system is "down," the new software is "buggy," your hard drive just crashed, your modem's not working, or you are infected with the latest virus, a computer crises is a superb dodging crutch.

CHAPTER 10

Physical Escapes

Diplomacy is the art of saying "nice doggie"
until you can find a rock.
—WILL ROGERS

No matter how good you are with words, how silver-tongued you are when lying, and how vast your reservoir of excuses, there is nothing as liberating as a well-enacted physical dodge. In fact, if you are face-to-face with trouble, your self-preservation may depend on your putting your whole body into your escape. You can't hang up on someone in person. When some lowlife you just met is about to throw his arms around you or you realize the person sitting next to you on the plane is a proselytizing religious zealot, what you are having is a physical problem, which often requires a physical solution.

THE SHAKE AND BREAK

Let's say you are attending what is supposed to be a fascinating weekend symposium on cosmic evolution and you are stuck with someone who is talking nonstop about his son's latest track victory. You want out of this conversation badly, but you can't think of what to do—especially as you can't get a word in edgewise. Don't panic. Just follow these simple steps:

Step one: As you are smiling at what this proud papa is saying, stick your hand out until he instinctively takes it, or just grab his gesticulating hand.

Step two: Shake the hand until its owner either stops speaking or at least slows down.

Step three: Smile more warmly, and say something like, "It's been so nice meeting [talking with] you!"

Step four: Turn and walk away.

(Obviously, if the World's Proudest Dad has a drink in one hand and a plate in the other, you will not be able to perform the Shake and Break unless he is close enough to a table and you are forceful enough to inspire him to set something down.)

This technique can also be used to duck an unwanted goodnight kiss. Just be certain to put out your hand before your amorous date gets too far into his pre-kiss lean. Then Shake—and Break!

The Human Sacrifice, which many people use without realizing it, has always been a favorite technique among my readers. It's a clever maneuver because it poses as a social grace. As long as there are other people around, you can use it to escape from a bore, a creep, or a boozer—or even just to dodge an unwanted hello kiss.

There you are, stuck in the conversation from hell. Before your mind numbs out completely, look around you and find someone to serve as your sacrifice. Proximity is important. You have to be able to reach out and grab this third person, who must be someone you either know or have met. Then you pull that person into your little twosome. Immediately you will feel a shift, a loosening of the bore's hold on you. Introduce the new person to the bore in a way that implies you are just being a good mingler by introducing two people who will probably have a lot in common. *As soon as their eyes meet,* get out of there. Immediately. You must fade out of the conversation within twenty seconds or this conversational change of partners will not work. A pleasant "Excuse me" will suffice as your parting. As in ballroom dancing, you can't be considered rude, since you have procured a new partner before moving on.

If you want to use the Human Sacrifice to avoiding a greeting kiss, you need some luck and very good timing. Your sacrifice has to be strategically located at the exact moment of the impending kiss. Then you need to quickly thrust the third person in between you and the incoming smooch, in what should look like an impulsive introduction. Frankly I have rarely seen

this done with grace. (But I have often seen it performed somewhat clumsily and it still gets the job done.)

BRUISING FOR CRUISING

If there is no one around to save you, you may have to get
violent. Not to others, but to yourself. This trick—which admittedly does take some amount of playacting—is based on the
concept that if someone thinks you are in pain (physical, not
just psychological) you can be excused for having no manners—
that is, for walking away when he is in the middle of a sentence.
Even the most self-involved bore will not expect you to stay
and listen to him when you are doubled over in agony. But
remember: You're supposed to be faking it. Try not to actually
hurt yourself.

Here are some self-inflicted injuries or sudden maladies you
can try:

cramps
biting your tongue
biting down on your fork
hitting your shin on the coffee table
unexpected wave of nausea
turned ankle
something painful in your eye
shooting pain in your temple
back spasm
spilling something on yourself (while it is not an actual
    injury, this garners the same result—your exit in
    order to deal with your now-soiled clothing)

After you have expressed your discomfort—with anything from a silent but visible cringe to a piercing scream—excuse yourself and leave. If the person offers to come help you, wave him away with "Please, it's not necessary, *do* excuse me." Or even, "Better keep away from me—I'm a walking disaster."

HOW TO VANISH INTO THIN AIR

In certain situations, there is nothing we long for so much as the ability to magically disappear. I think people love *Star Trek* primarily for that wonderful transporter on the *Enterprise*. I can't tell you how many times have I wanted Scotty to beam *me* up. But until the world's molecule-scrambling technology can offer us actual evaporation, here are some useful maneuvers:

DODGE BALL: You are at a cocktail party, having a quiet moment alone, sipping your martini, and surveying the mingling field. Suddenly you notice a new arrival to the party. It's a woman you absolutely abhor. Every time you see her she insists on gossiping about other people who are present. When she makes eye contact with you, you just know she is thinking of heading your way.

You've got to be quick on your feet to succeed at Dodge Ball. As soon as you see this woman glance at you, you must not hesitate—not even for a microsecond. You don't smile at her; in fact, you try to act as if you haven't seen her. You then make a beeline for a cluster of people whom know you and who will let you into their protective custody, fast.

THE FADE-OUT: You are still at the cocktail party, but now the Gossip has somehow contrived to join the same group you entered to get away from her. Right now everyone is involved in a lively discussion about "Sex and the City," but you are afraid that once this topic peters out people will start to peel off, and you could be left alone with the Gossip after all. You decide the best thing to do is for you to Fade Out as soon as you can.

Here's how: Wait until no one is talking to you or looking at you too closely, and then, ever so slowly, start to inch backward. Stay alert as you begin your disappearing act, just in case the conversation should turn back to you in mid-fade (in which case you must abort your Fade-Out). When you think you are far enough away from the group, you can allow your head to turn as if your attention has been caught by something or someone. Then walk quickly away, as if you were never really with the group in the first place.

USING PROPS

One woman I interviewed, Diane, was so excited about her first trip to Italy that she got on the plane without giving a thought to travel protection. I don't mean travel insurance or life vests. I am talking about *dodging protection*. As any veteran traveler knows, artful dodging is often required when you are traveling—in spite of the fact that you are usually stuck in your seat. Diane learned this fact of life the hard way when she found herself seated next to a woman who thought of herself as Ann Landers, Dear Abby, Miss Manners, and Eloise all rolled into one. She gave nonstop advice. Diane had nothing to fend off this woman but a half-hearted attempt at sleeping—which didn't work.

For deflecting unwanted conversation during travel, you must have the right props. Here are provisions for the artful dodger on the road, listed in order of importance:

AUDIO ARMOR: Bring a Walkman or CD player. It doesn't have to be a real one. In fact, all you really need are the earphones, with a wire running into a bag that looks as if it could contain an audio device.

READING MATERIAL: Forget newspapers. Newspapers are just as likely to inspire conversation as they are to discourage it. Magazines are sometimes adequate but I wouldn't count on their warding off a seatmate who really wants to talk. What you really need is a book, and unfortunately for your carrying comfort, it should be a thick book. The bigger the book, the more effective the dodge. People tend to think your reading is more important if it is something heavy, proving once again that books are in fact judged by their covers.

THE SCONE OF SILENCE: I know someone who traveled through Europe by train, and almost always got his own compartment. How he did it was like this: He would fill a large empty scotch bottle with iced tea, and when anyone opened the door to his compartment, there he would be, slouched on the seat, guzzling his "scotch."

Offputting food or drink can repel strangers. Try eating something messy while you stare out the window. Scones are good because they are usually dry and crumbly, making it difficult to do anything but mumble an answer, and making you look like a slob. You can use the Scone of Silence not just for travel dodges but also for dodging lustful dates (most people won't kiss you—at least not for the first time—while you are stuffing your face), for avoiding conversation at work ("Lemme finish chewing") or even for deterring anger ("Don't yell at me! . . . Here, eat this!").

SUNGLASSES: This might sound odd, and it's hard to pull off if it's a night flight, but sunglasses can protect you from eye contact with your travel mates. Conversations hardly ever get started without eye contact. Have the sunglasses on when you enter the plane; if you sit next to Adonis, you can always remove them (slowly and seductively).

ELUDING ELEVATOR ADVANCES AND OTHER TIGHT-QUARTER QUANDARIES

Houdini used to extricate himself from locked coffins and trunks, inside which he was tied up in ropes and straitjackets. I try to invoke the spirit of Houdini every time I feel trapped with someone undesirable in a confined space.

I don't know whether it's just me, but I seem to have a problem with people in elevators. I have on occasion had to physically push people away from me in elevators, which is an unpleasant, very nonartful thing to have to do. Certain people can get very aggressive when they are in an enclosed space with you. Some hunting instinct must tell them that since you have no place to run they must give chase.

My friends Nick and Pat have a different kind of elevator

problem. They have a truly crazy neighbor who, whenever he gets in the elevator with them, tries very hard to engage them, by inviting them to events, telling them bizarre stories about his life, and asking for help and advice. Nick and Pat are afraid of offending him because they feel there is a possibility that he is truly dangerous. For this reason they do not want to overtly avoid getting into the elevator with him.

Believe it or not there are several effective techniques for keeping elevator nuisances at bay. 1) If a person starts getting too close to you and is behaving as if any minute he is going to physically pounce, make an exaggerated, startled movement backward, while raising your hands slightly up in front of you. If he didn't realize what he was doing this brings him to his senses, and if he did realize what he was doing it tells him you are aware of it and are *not into it*. 2) For psychological assaults in elevators—for Nick and Pat's problem, for example—the best defense is offense. I have found the only way to deflect a major nut is with some nuttiness of your own. Instead of answering him, keep looking at your watch and shaking your head and muttering, "Damn." Act as if you are so self-absorbed you can't really even hear him. If he demands your attention by repeatedly asking direct questions and touching you on the arm, nod briefly or say things like "yeah . . ." "maybe . . ." and "I don't know . . ." before getting right back to your own angst. 3) Use the "I forgot something" excuse whenever you are really nervous about the elevator ride. You can remember something you forgot right before you get on the elevator (after you have seen who is already in it); or you can remember halfway down and get off on the wrong floor on purpose (when you suspect he's an authentic masher).

Similar dodging dilemmas present themselves on crowded subway trains. One person I interviewed, a man named James, told me about a superslick maneuver he frequently uses on the subway. Like many people, he likes to read on his way to work; unfortunately, there are other people who like to *talk* on their way to work. Now, James is a very nice guy who can't stand to be discourteous. Whenever he finds himself drawn into one of these unlooked-for conversations, he waits for the train to pull into a station and pretends that he is at his destination. He says good-bye to the talkative stranger, then exits that subway car, runs down the platform, and gets on another car before the doors close. (If he's lucky, this time he finds a seat next to a fellow reader.)

THE INVISIBLE MAN

There are many valid reasons for wanting to be invisible. If you are a celebrity you don't want to be bothered on the street. If you live in the same neighborhood as your employer or co-workers you may not want to socialize with them outside of work. If you are in a very bad mood you might just not want to talk to *anyone* until it lifts. If you are like me, sometimes you just don't want anyone you know to see you in ripped sweats and a stained T-shirt. Here are a few tips to help you in your pursuit of invisibility.

DISGUISES: Don't balk at the idea of a disguise. It doesn't have to be a Groucho nose. Big hats, sunglasses—even a wig—are great for dodging the world at large. A more subtle way of disguising yourself is to wear clothes you wouldn't normally wear.

INVISIBLE THINKING: Most people are not going to plan ahead enough to be wearing a disguise. But when you see someone coming whom you don't feel like talking to, you can mentally make yourself invisible. Make yourself small. Look down at your newspaper, at your feet, at the pavement. Become engrossed in the label on a can of soup in the grocery store. Walk very fast, and look as if you are contemplating something urgent. Looking busy and distracted can sometimes even give you invisibility at the office.

USING YOUR SURROUNDINGS: I have a friend whose place of work is what I call the Palace of Dodging. He works as a teacher, in one school but in two different departments. At any given time there are five places he can legitimately be. No one can ever find him. His wife has given up trying to reach him at work because he is so hard to locate. He has achieved almost total invisibility. In short, he has found a habitat where, once inside, there is no need for artful dodging—it's effortless dodging.

CHAPTER 11

Expert Only Dodges

It's kind of fun to do the impossible.
—WALT DISNEY

When you are ready to give your dodging muscles a real workout, try using one of the advanced techniques below. They are high-risk maneuvers, but when you pull them off it can be very satisfying. Moreover, an expert dodge may be your only hope if you are in really big trouble. If you've just been caught vacationing in Florida by your boss when you are supposed to be at a business meeting in London, you may as well pull out all the stops.

DAREDEVIL DODGING: THE WILD STORY

My favorite Wild Story comes from one of my poker buddies (I'll call her Debbie). About ten years ago Debbie went to Paris to visit her boyfriend. Because she was young—and because she is Debbie—upon arriving in Paris she fell immediately in lust with her boyfriend's best friend. He had an apartment around the corner from the boyfriend. Debbie started going back and forth between the two apartments, hoping the boyfriend wouldn't find out.

Of course, the boyfriend not only found out but caught them *in flagrante*. He began to yell and cry and threaten. What did Debbie do? She sat them both down and very gravely informed them that her injudicious behavior was due to her having leukemia. In fact, she told them, she had less than a year to live. So couldn't they forgive her for sowing a few oats?

According to Debbie, they both bought her story. Not only that, but she accidentally ran into one of them a year ago, and when he expressed shock at seeing her, she joyfully told him she was in remission!

The theory behind the Wild Story is that people will accept it because they can't believe you would make up an excuse that bizarre or extreme. Many Wild Stories are just classic excuses with some very unusual or dramatic additions. It's always best if you make up your own Wild Story out of the bits and pieces of your own experience; it sounds more authentic that way. However, here are some sample Wild Stories—ones people have actually used with success—to get you started: (**Note:** The Wild Story, like a good joke, must be told well. Be sure to add as many details as you can.)

THE PET PYTHON: You couldn't do your assignment because your boyfriend's pet python was sitting on the papers (or sitting on the book) and wouldn't move.

THE CASE OF THE FLYING LADY: The reason you never showed up at the important meeting is because on your way to it, you were hit by a flying woman. The woman had been hit by a bus as she was crossing the street. The bus caused her to fly up into the air, hitting you during her descent. You were knocked over and, though you had only minor injuries, the police made you go along with the woman to the hospital.

UP IN SMOKE: The contract was sitting on your desk. Someone left a cigarette smoldering in your ashtray (which you didn't notice since you never use it). Your papers caught on fire and the contract burned to a crisp.

HIT BY PLASTIC: You were driving on the highway when a plastic bag hit your windshield and you drove into a ditch.

PARENTAL PANIC: You were about to leave for work when your eight-year-old kid came to you and said, "Daddy? Is it all right if I smoke marijuana today on the playground like the other kids?"

THE FLOOD: You were walking out the door to come to the birthday party when your washing machine broke down. The water started gushing out. You just now found the tap to shut the water off, but your kitchen looks like a swimming pool.

CULT WEEKEND: You are sorry you didn't get your work done, but you went to what you thought was going to be a nice weekend in the country with a friend and it turned out to be a cult gathering. . . . They kept you up all weekend and didn't feed you and tried to convert you. You barely escaped.

The perpetrator of the Wild Story succeeds for the same reason a magician does. He entertains and/or mesmerizes the audience as he performs his trick. The audience enjoys the story so much they really *want* to believe it; it adds color to their humdrum day.

THE GREAT GUILT GAMBIT*

Your boss has asked you to write up a proposal for a new project. She wants it on her desk by Friday. Friday arrives and you haven't done it—in fact you haven't even started. Your boss appears at your door. "Where's that proposal?" she says. You look stumped. "Oh no," you say. You lean back in your chair, eyes closed. You put your hand on your stomach as if you are in pain. Groan some. Look like you are going to die. "I can't believe I forgot you wanted that today. I'll stay home this weekend—even though we were planning a trip with the kids—but I'll have it to you by Monday. I am so sorry. . . ." With any luck the anger on your boss's face will soon change to concern—and then, hopefully, after a little more self-loathing from you—guilt. "Never mind," she'll say, "it's not that big a deal. Next week sometime is fine. Are you okay?"

Of course, as in Russian Roulette, you have to be prepared

*Please consult a licensed therapist before using this dodge.

for this plot to backfire in the way only an expert dodge can—a major way. You could be spending the weekend at the office.

PLAYING CHICKEN

Remember James Dean in *Rebel Without a Cause,* racing with another teen, driving his car as fast as he could toward the edge of a cliff? The way this potentially fatal game was played in the movie, the last person to jump out of the car before it goes off the cliff was the chicken. If you have nerves of steel or are feeling reckless you might want to try the artful dodger's version of this daring feat. It can be used to get out of social events that you feel a very strong obligation to attend.

Ready? Start your engines. Call up the person in charge of the event. Get detailed directions, tell her you are looking forward to it. Call again to ask what you can bring. Up until the very last minute, illustrate that you are absolutely planning on being there. You are heading for the get-together at high speed. Then, at the very last minute, you bail. You just don't show up, or you call five minutes before to cancel. Later you carry on at great length about how you can't believe that after all that anticipation you didn't make it, due to your old friend from Mexico showing up on your doorstep (or any other excuse you want to use). The bigger a show you make about coming, the less suspicious the host will be that you were planning to ditch all along.

(**Note:** Do not use this technique if you are supposed to meet only one person. That would constitute a stand-up, and that is a dodging sin.)

THE "POOR ME" PLOY

Like many of these advanced dodging techniques, the "Poor Me" Ploy requires a devotion to artful dodging that borders on the pathological. Nevertheless, there is no question that it can be a very effective technique.

I worked with someone once who had this pity act down pat. Every day he would sit at his desk, looking down in the mouth, stressed out, overwrought, and extremely put upon. He constantly moaned about how overworked he was. He projected this attitude so convincingly that people actually gave him less work to do. On the other hand, my cheery how-can-I-help-you stance was rewarded by my getting more than my share of assignments. It wasn't until I saw the "Poor Me" man outside the office on a Saturday, whistling a little tune and smiling away, that I realized he was enacting a highly sophisticated—and borderline diabolical—permanent preemptive dodge at work.

Similar in style to the Mysterious Melodrama (page 79), the "Poor Me" Ploy will not win you any popularity contests, but in certain kinds of jobs it can keep extra work away from you. If you project a constant "I'm so overworked" aura, people will, consciously or unconsciously, tend to not want to add to your load. This "I'm closed for business!" attitude can be conveyed to some degree over the phone as well. Many people deflect further demands on their time by answering the phone as if they were in the middle of a crisis. My own grandfather used to answer the phone with a shouted "What do you want?"—making people afraid to want anything at all.

STRANGER IN A STRANGE LAND

You need to have an ear for at least one foreign language and a large amount of bravado to pull this one off, but if you do it's a positively 100 percent successful dodge. Best used when traveling or out in public (among strangers), Stranger in a Strange Land is the pretense that you do not speak English. You can either use a thick accent over broken English ("No speak anglais . . .") or have a few sentences you can say really well in the other language. Naturally, if you are fluent in another language you will have an easier time of it. But no old Hollywood accents please ("I-a No-a Speak-a Da English-a")! You can never let anyone know you would go to such lengths to avoid speaking to him.

(**Warning:** Do not play Stranger in a Strange Land unless you are relatively sure the other person doesn't speak "your" language. For example, in Little Italy, Italian won't do.)

THE OFFENSIVE DODGE

Frankly, this kind of dodging is not my style. It's—well—it's offensive. But it suits some people because it is a take-control kind of move. It's proactive. If you are the kind of person who likes to actually go after people and smash into them on the bumper car ride at the amusement park (interestingly enough, a ride that was called Dodgem in the 1920s) rather than try to avoid being hit, you might like Offensive dodging.

Here's an example: You have invited a woman to your house for dinner. The night before she is supposed to come, you have second thoughts about the whole deal and you want to back out of it. You call her up and tell her you are looking forward to having her over, but that you just wanted her to know you have to watch professional wrestling during her visit. You also tell her a few of your buddies might drop by. If that doesn't persuade her to cancel, you ask her if she wouldn't mind trying to get the ring out of your bath tub while she is over—that it's a girl thing and you can't deal with it.

There are countless ways to make someone go away by being repulsive, boring, loud, scary, or strange. You can stare at one point on a person's face until she gets so unnerved she goes away. You can grab someone's hand and kiss it passionately—especially if it's a man and he is in the middle of talking about mutual funds. You can let on that you have a bad virus and say, "I don't *think* I'm contagious." The point of Offensive dodging is to force the other person to dodge *you*—by showing yourself to be totally undesirable—leaving you guilt- and blame-free. Needless to say, it takes a special person to purposefully make people despise him.

THE EXORCIST

There are some problems that just won't go away, and there are some people who refuse to take a hint. When you sense a suitor has become a stalker, or a houseguest has become a permanent fixture, you may have to go beyond normal dodging methods to have any real effect. Get ready to commit some of the Seven Dodging Sins. This technique deals with things that go beyond dodging—for those times you feel that the interaction between you and the dodgee is no longer a dance. It's war.

Burning Your Bridges

You've really had it with two of your friends. Actually they are your ex-husband's college fraternity buddies, but somehow you ended up with them in the divorce settlement. They often show up unannounced, mess up your clean kitchen, hog the remote, and never want to leave. *That's it*, you finally think to yourself one day after they used your toothbrush to play fetch with the dog, *I am ready to burn my bridges*.

The next time they come over and do not leave at a decent hour, you send them out for beer. As soon as they leave, you turn out the lights, lock all the doors, and go to bed. When (after pounding on the door for a while) they realize you are mad at them and they want to make it up to you by taking you to lunch the next day, you tell them to meet you at a certain restaurant and then you don't show up. When you run into them at the mall about a month later, you tell them you are now living with a new man who gets jealous if you have any other male friends.

Playing Dead

My friend Marla was forced to do this with a man she met through the personals. She went out with him exactly three times. (She thought he was creepy from the beginning but Marla has a three-date rule she likes to follow.) When she told him at the end of the third date he wasn't her type, he smiled strangely and said, "Oh I know your type, baby." This was not a good sign. Sure enough, he started calling her every day, sometimes in the middle of the night. She told him she was busy, she told him she was dating someone else, she told him she was gay—nothing worked. Occasionally when she was out on another date she would discover he had been following her. She tried to tell him this made her uncomfortable and had to stop, but he would counter her objections with protestations of love—complete with poetry. She tried every dodge she could think of and then finally—she gave up and Played Dead.

When you Play Dead you go underground; you don't return the person's phone calls or E-mail. (You can't answer your phone for a while, so make sure your machine is working and tell your friends you are screening your calls.) You don't respond to gifts or letters. It's a campaign of total ignoring—the Deaf and Dumb dodge taken to extremes. If you see him on the street, you act as if he is not there. Eventually, unless you are dealing with someone truly insane, this absolute disengagement will work.

A woman I was interviewing had a similar problem, though less dramatic. She has been married for ten years but has a former boyfriend who will periodically write to her, claiming he is still in love with her, making veiled threats of suicide, and asking if he can come for a visit. He says he understands and respects the fact that she is married. The woman told me that after she broke up with him, she would notice him following her sometimes. He even convinced her to go see his therapist with him. (The therapist told her she was being manipulated by the man.) But that was twelve years ago.

"And you still have contact with this guy?" I asked, incredulous.

"Well," she told me, "I feel sorry for him and he always seems so lost. . . ."

"Not lost enough," I said to her. I told her that unless she wanted to keep the relationship with this pseudo-stalker alive, she needed to Play Dead. (And dead people don't return phone calls or answer letters.)

❧

The Anti-Dodge:
Calling in Well

So. You've learned how to artfully avoid, evade, and evict anyone and everyone in your life. You've practiced your preemptive dodging, perfected the Duck and Cover, and mastered the Absentminded Professor. I've instructed you thoroughly in the controversial craft of lying through your teeth (and every other part of your body) and explained exactly why it is that subterfuge is prized among people in polite society. Now fasten your seat belts because I am going to completely contradict myself by telling you that there *are* times when it is better to be utterly and unabashedly honest.

I think of this non-technique as the anti-dodge because it is the polar opposite of dodging. Mind you, it is still artful. And you still get to avoid whatever it is you don't want to do or haven't done. But it it not a dodge. It is a guilt-free, fear-free, anger-free, angst-free "no thank-you."

You usually cannot fake this one. You have to really feel it. And frankly, you may have to have a lot of a psychotherapy before you can do it at all. Unlike the stiff refusal of the man who had sworn off greeting kisses (see page xiii), your serene turndown must be untainted by any negative feeling. "I woke up this morning and saw the sun shining and told myself I was going to take the day off today! And that is just what I am doing," you might announce to your boss, without fear of how he will respond. Or, if you are in anti-dodge mode and you are turning down a date, you say, "The truth is that I don't want to go out with you; we have too little in common and I'm going to keep looking for someone who is right for me. But I wish you good luck and happiness."

People are often disarmed, even charmed, when you confidently and unapologetically tell the truth about why you are not coming, why you are late, or why you are not prepared. *But only if you yourself feel absolutely no guilt.* The essential element of the anti-dodge is the projection of sincere love and calm. As with walking on hot coals, if you think you are going to get burned, you will!

Of course, you may occasionally get a bad response to your straight-from-the-heart communication. ("Oh yeah? Well *I* woke up today and said to myself, 'I'm going to fire someone today!' ") But believe it or not, if you are truly clear and confident about what you are saying, this usually won't happen. The person on the other end of your non-dodge will probably say something like "Oh . . . well . . . that's fine," even as he is wondering to himself just why it is he isn't angrier. The secret? Your no-fear energy has infected him!

One last piece advice: Never forget that before you opt for

any kind of dodging, anti or otherwise, you should consider the possibility that the event or person you are poised to push away could end up being a plus in your life. How many times have we said to ourselves after a party, "If I hadn't gone to that ghastly thing I would never have met so-and-so?" How often have we ducked a difficult phone call for days, until finally taking it and realizing it wasn't so difficult after all—that in fact it was rewarding? Life is filled with opportunities, challenges, and experiences; become too frequent a dodger and you may forget that dodging was invented to make you freer, not to shut out the world.

Well, not the whole world, anyway. Inevitably, you will occasionally need to shut out *part* of the world. But now that you have access to the artful dodger's bag of tricks, you will be able to show consideration for others as you do it; you can dodge unto others as you would have them dodge unto you.

In other words, you can pull the wool over their eyes so gently they'll never see you heading for the exit.

INDEX